PREPARATION FOR PARENTHOOD

How To Create A Nurturing Family

DONNA EWY

With a Foreword by Elisabeth Bing

A PLUME BOOK

NEW AMERICAN LIBRARY

NEW YORK AND SCARBOROUGH, ONTARIO

NAL BOOKS ARE AVAILABLE AT QUANTITY DISCOUNTS WHEN USED TO
PROMOTE PRODUCTS OR SERVICES. FOR INFORMATION PLEASE WRITE TO
PREMIUM MARKETING DIVISION, NEW AMERICAN LIBRARY,
1633 BROADWAY, NEW YORK, NEW YORK 10019.

SIGNET, SIGNET CLASSIC, MENTOR, PLUME, MERIDIAN AND NAL BOOKS
are published in the United States by New American Library,
1633 Broadway, New York, New York 10019,
in Canada by The New American Library of Canada Limited,
81 Mack Avenue, Scarborough, Ontario M1L 1M8

Library of Congress Cataloging in Publication Data

Ewy, Donna.
    Preparation for parenthood.

    Bibliography
    Includes index.
    1. Parenthood.   2. Parent and child.   3. Family.
I. Title.
HQ755.8.E975 1985   306.8'74   85-10463
ISBN 0-452-25691-7

First Printing, July, 1985

1   2   3   4   5   6   7   8   9

PRINTED IN THE UNITED STATES OF AMERICA

Dedicated to Danielle Elizabeth Mallinson,
the little angel who sat on my shoulder and
helped me write this book, and to her loving
family who inspired me to finish it.

CONTENTS

FOREWORD

Parenthood is a task that most of us want to experience one day. Building and nurturing a healthy and happy family is the goal we hope to achieve.

Reading Donna Ewy's excellently organized book on the family, I relived my own childhood—and parenthood—and recognized her sympathetic understanding of all the phases of growing up in a family, as a child and later as a parent. Chapter by chapter I nodded and said to myself, "Yes, it's just like that, step by step."

I was number four of five children, and I know that at the time, or most of the time, I did not question whether it would be better to be higher or lower on the totem pole. Nevertheless, I also remember wishing occasionally that I could have all the attention and advantages the youngest in the family seemed to get. I remember my younger brother wanting me to play with him and his getting angry with me and crying if I wanted to play with children my own age. Seeing him upset, our babysitter would often shake me and exclaim angrily, "You naughty girl, what are you doing to make your little brother cry so bitterly?" I felt at such moments that the world was very unjust and adults without any understanding of children.

And at other times, I was envious of my older sisters or brother. They could accompany my mother when she went shopping. How I wished she had asked me for some reason or other to come along and help carry the shopping bags. And how annoying it was that I always had to wear my sisters' outgrown dresses. It was not until I was fourteen years old that I was allowed to have my own new outfit for my confirmation—a lovely velveteen dress.

As I look at these childhood memories, they seem now very small, almost insignificant, compared with other exciting things I remember so well:

My parents' constant interest in all my everyday experiences, their sharing in my sorrows and joys, the stimulation I received from them with regard to schoolwork and lots and lots of extracurricular learning. I remember well our bicycle trips, the seven of us with knapsacks on our backs, riding into the woods.

I don't know whether my parents followed any particular theories or rules in educating us, or whether they brought us up the way they did because they had an unfailing instinct as to how to create a stimulating and harmonious family.

I do know that many, many years later, when I gave birth to my own son, I was quite determined to continue my parents' wonderful feeling and understanding for their children, and their unerring support of all of us at the right times.

Every parent—and future parent—can benefit from reading Donna Ewy's comprehensive book on how to create and nurture a family.

I met Donna's family in their own home and when they were in New York on a visit, and I can report that she follows in practice the advice she gives us in her book.

—Elisabeth Bing, ACCE
New York

A PERSONAL NOTE

Not many years ago, I had four babies all under five and all in diapers. I didn't have the time or energy to read books on parenting—let alone make conscious decisions. I was in over my head and felt lucky just to get food on the table, clothes washed, noses wiped, and buttons buttoned. I certainly never had time to worry about creativity and ego identity.

When our first daughter, Margot, was born I had tried to be what I thought was the "perfect mother" and even took pride and joy in ironing her nightgowns and socks. By the time the last child, Leon, was born, he was lucky to get two socks—and to this day, he still doesn't know that socks are supposed to be the same color.

When my first child said, "I hate you," I went into paroxysms of guilt. "Where did I go wrong?" When the last child said, "I hate you," I said, "What else is new?" When the second child said, "I didn't ask to be born," I went into a long detailed discussion on eggs and sperm. When the third child said, "I didn't ask to be born," I told him I found him in a cabbage patch, and he had begged me to take him home into our family.

Now when I read an article about parenting I think, "Oh, my God, how did my children ever turn out normal?" Even as I was writing this book, I was swept by tides of guilt. I've begged forgiveness from my first daughter for all the wrongs I did her in my innocence and lack of experience. From my second daughter I have asked forgiveness for not giving her enough attention, wedged as she was between an older sister and a younger brother. To my third child, I have apologized for not even knowing where he was half the time. And, from the last-born, I have asked forgiveness for any ostracism he may have suffered among his peers for mismatched socks.

Yet somehow, despite my imperfections as a parent, they all turned out to be trusting, independent, creative, industrious human beings who are wonderfully spontaneous and loving individuals. Margot is working on a graduate degree in education. Suzanne is looking at graduate work in French. Rodger is in his second year at the university in business and works full-time in a stock brokerage firm. Leon, his brother, has special talents in physics, mathematics, and the classics. They are all thinking about what kind of parents they are going to be and what things we did for them that they want (and don't want) to pass on to their own children.

I guess the moral of this story is that parenting may seem to be an overwhelming task to be taken on only by the hardiest—and in fact, a parent can make many many mistakes—but with love and humor, the human child is tough and resilient.

I thank my family for their wonderful contributions to this book. The children contributed their experiences as they took us from the honeymoon phase, through the shock of adding an infant to our lives; through the crisis of the independent toddler; into the play age, where they blabbed all the family secrets to anyone who would listen; past school age, where teachers judged us by how "well" our children did in school; right into adolescence, where their friends judged us by the horror stories our children told them about us; into launching them into the world—which rocked our family as much as any phase. I also thank them for contributing their skills to this book. Rodger gave suggestions while Suzy edited and critiqued the first draft. Leon typed and edited the final draft. And Margot proofread as it came off the typewriter.

I thank Rodger, the father, for his support and love for the family throughout the years. It hasn't been easy, but we feel that it's about the greatest accomplishment anyone could ever wish for.

INTRODUCTION

"We started out sure that our marriage would be the perfect marriage. We would beat all odds and have the perfect family with the perfect kids. Somewhere along the way, the bubble burst," said Anita, a young mother of three children, during a family counseling session. "We found ourselves to be ordinary human beings married to ordinary mortals. Our marriage had its ups and downs. Our kids were no more or less perfect than we. Sure, we had our joys, but we've also had our share of pain. I wish someone had told us what it all was really about."

Again and again I have seen people like Anita in all phases of marriage echoing the theme of innocence fading and expressing their needs for realistic insights and skills.

While every family starts out hoping to be loving and happy, statistics show that marriages and families are failing at an alarming rate. Never before in history have our chances for joy seemed so great. But the family seems suddenly to have gone out of control. Half of all marriages end in divorce. The incidence of child abuse is frightening. The numbers of teenage drug abusers, suicides, pregnancies, delinquents, and runaways are unprecedented.

What is happening?

The newly married couple go into parenthood with Sleeping Beauty and Prince Charming expectations: expecting to live the perfect life happily ever after. When they find that the normal pathways of life are filled with stresses and crises at each stage, they are ill prepared to cope with marriage, let alone parenthood.

During preparation for my doctoral dissertation on family communications, it became clear that although there has been a great deal of exciting and important research in marriage and family therapy to counsel families in trouble, little of this new information has filtered down to the lay person who needs it.

I had been married for twenty years, had conceived, given birth, and raised four energetic, wonderful and complex human beings, only after having crossed many rivers of troubled waters. While studying family dynamics and therapy, I would come home and think: "If I had been aware of this information twenty years ago, I could have avoided some of those muddy rivers, ridden the waves, and even had a little fun along the way."

I regretted not having this information while raising four teenagers. I learned that they were doing what nature's biological time clock had planned for them, and I was bucking them all the way, although with each succeeding child I became more relaxed, trusted their strengths more, and let go earlier. The earlier the child reached maturity, the easier my parenting job had been.

As I delved deeper into my studies, while at the same time counseling other families and parenting my own four, I became convinced that the family can not only survive but even have fun if normal stresses can be used as tools of growth rather than instruments of destruction. The more parents know about normal development and the more they learn to nurture the wonderful potential resources of the human being, the more pleasant and healthy their family can become.

And so, that is what this book is about: the nurturing family, how it develops, what stages it goes through, and how it handles the normal but seemingly unpredictable stresses of life. With this knowledge, it will be easier for you to have a family that can communicate, show appreciation, have fun, forgive each other, accept things that cannot be changed, and finally simply "tough out" hard times and hold on until they're better.

This book is based on the lives of many families who have

shared their stories, their pains and their joys. It includes lessons I have learned from my own large, extended family, and from my own children, who have tried and tested me and given me humility and great respect for the depth and profundity of the human race. The book is also based on lessons I have learned from families I have counseled.

Over three thousand people throughout North America and Europe have responded to questionnaires from workshops I gave on the nurturing family; they generously contributed their life experiences to help me write this book. Some of the examples come from families I have worked with as Director of Youth Programs with the YMCA low-income, high-risk adolescent program. In all cases the names and backgrounds have been changed and their unique experiences have been blended into composites that do not describe any one family, but form a story of the human family. The families who have shared with us come from all walks of life; they are of many nationalities and of all economic classes. Some are traditional two-parent families, others are single-parent families. In some, the mother has an outside occupation, while in others the mothers stays home. Some are traditional extended families, others are nuclear and isolated, and still others, through divorce or death of a spouse, have blended families.

Families need handling with care. Any family can lose control at any point in the family cycle. Some will turn to professional help. Yet most families have the capacity to work through crises and transitions without help if they have the basic knowledge and skills, and the comforting understanding that they are not alone. And when confronted and solved, problems can give families strength, courage, and skills needed to thrive throughout the coming generations.

You have three basic tasks in family life: to nurture yourself, to nurture your marriage, and to nurture your children. Your goal is to ensure that each member of the family has the love and protection he or she needs to develop a strong sense of self and self-esteem and eventually to become a productive and creative member of society—an adult who can, in turn, parent healthy children.

For your family to have a fulfilling, intimate relationship without its members losing their sense of self, it is important that you understand how families work and how to enhance the potential strengths and resources within your family unit.

I wrote this book to help you nurture a loving, happy family. Part I, Family Stages, will help you anticipate the many challenges that are a normal part of family living. Part II, Family Skills, will help you cope with them.

PREPARATION FOR PARENTHOOD

PART I

FAMILY STAGES

1

THE MAKING
OF A HEALTHY
HUMAN BEING

Children are born with their own unique strengths and weaknesses. You as parents do not really make or break your children; rather, you help shape them by providing a trusting and loving environment in which their physical, emotional, social, and psychological potential can unfold naturally.

If you recognize that children mature largely according to an inner timetable, your job as a parent will seem much easier. Every child has a built-in biological time clock, and, *with guidance*, can be trusted to obey inner laws of development, even though there are optimum experiences which you can provide your children to help them develop self-esteem, creativity, and spontaneity and discern the joy of living.

The noted psychologist Erik Erikson says, "If only we will learn to let live, the plan for growth is all there." For the parent, however, this concept can raise many questions.

How can you enjoy the unfolding of your children? How can you feel confident in tuning into and following your children's inner timetable? How do you know what guidance they need? Is it all right for you to hold your child when it seems best for him or her, to smile when your baby smiles, to follow your child's readiness to walk or be toilet-trained?

How do you resist your natural temptation to encourage your child to do things faster than he or she may be willing to? How do you make room for your child's individuality, and avoid

comparing him or her to other children? How can you handle
the temptation to take out your own frustrations and unresolved
problems on your child and to dominate your child because
you feel helpless yourself? How best can you respond to your
child's own capacities and inclinations rather than trying to
shape him or her into the person you yourself wanted to be?

What Kind of Parent Are You Likely to Be?

Parenting is a complex business. There is no single positive
factor that determines your parenting style. There are some
major factors, however, which will influence it: your own personality and development; your family of origin; your position
in your family; your marriage; your child's personality; and your
family's developmental stage. You will be learning new adult
roles, fantasizing about your future, and searching for meaningful goals.

Near the end of your twenties you may get a little tired of
playing adult and want to relax. The husband may get tired of
what he is doing, and the wife may become bored. This may
be an upsetting time for the marriage.

During the thirties you will be busy settling down. This is
the time you usually are interested in finding your niche in the
professional world. You are no longer the new kid on the block.
While your family is young and growing, buying a house and
settling down may become a priority in your life.

As you enter the forties you may experience a sort of disquiet,
for you realize that you may not accomplish all of your dreams.
If your parents are aging, sick, or dying, you begin to recognize
your own mortality.

As you approach your fifties and your children begin to leave
home, you begin to accept your humanness and envision more
significant life goals. Love and compassion and helping the next
generation become much more interesting than making a mil-
lion dollars. You may be facing an awareness of your own physical decline as you see your children accelerating and blossoming
physically and sexually.

Family of Origin. The parenting you received as a child is a good indicator of how you will parent your own children. When you become a parent, both you and your parents will probably relive memories of your childhood. If you are dissatisfied with some of the ways in which you were parented, you can consciously choose a style you think would be better for your own children. Otherwise, you will pass on the practices and values of your own family.

Your Own Personality and Development. You were born with inherited characteristics that have been continually modified by your life experiences. How you feel about yourself, your confidence, your self-esteem, your ability to handle stress, and your need for attention are all essential parts of your personality.

You can expect your needs to change as you pass through your own adult developmental stages just as the needs of your children will change as they develop from infancy into adolescence. Your spouse and children will affect your psychological growth just as you will influence theirs. In early adulthood, you will be involved with cutting the invisible umbilical cord that ties you to your family of origin and developing a new home base.

Your Own Family Position. Research has shown that you are affected by the order in which you are born in the family. Sir Francis Galton showed that the oldest child is usually the achiever. Adler showed that birth order affects the personality development of the child as he or she strives for affection, attention, and acceptance. Toman showed that birth order also affects who the person chooses in marriage and the parenting patterns of each partner, as parents' expectations differ with each child.

In part, how you see yourself and how others see you are determined by your place in your own family of origin.

If you were the firstborn, you probably have struggles with power and control. If you choose a firstborn for a mate, you will probably have problems of power and dependence within your marriage. If you marry a second or middle child, your mate may have to deal with you in a forceful and dominant role. You will probably relate easily to your firstborn but perhaps need some help in understanding your second and middle children. You may be accustomed to having your way, and may have to take special care to share power and allow other members of your family to develop their own individuality.

If you are a second child in your family of origin, you may also have issues of power, self-esteem, and dependence to resolve. If you had a dominant older sibling you may have had to compensate by either giving in or manipulating to get your way. If you marry a firstborn you may find yourself reliving this pattern. As a submissive parent you might not give your children the support they need and you will probably have to work at sharing power. Your first child may be intimidating to you and you may find yourself very sympathetic to the second child. If you marry a second child, be sure that you and your mate give the family definite, clear rules and regulations they need to make sure you do not leave a dangerous power vacuum.

If you are a middle child you probably have resolved conflicts over power and independence. You may rebel if you marry a first child who tries to dominate you or have a baby who tries to manipulate you. If your spouse is another middle child, this combination has the best chance for success in that you both are used to leading when necessary, submitting to keep peace, and sharing power, although you may have difficulty understanding the power of your first child and the problems of your second.

If you are the baby in your family of origin, you are quite comfortable with getting what you want, and have developed a repertoire of techniques for handling others. You make a good partner to a dominant mate in that you seem to acquiesce, while at the same time, you know that you will get your own way. If you marry a second child, a middle child, or a baby, you may have to put special energy into making clear and concise rules for the family to live by. If you marry another baby, you all will probably have a great time, but will have to be careful not to leave a power vacuum.

Your Marriage. Another component of your parenting is your choice of spouse and the quality of your marriage as it passes through each of its own unique and important developmental stages. You will be choosing your mate and acquiring new in-laws in the first stage of marriage. During courtship and early marriage you both will be occupied with developing the values, goals, expectations, needs, and desires that make up your dream marriage.

With pregnancy come major adjustments. You will have less time and energy for the marriage, and the honeymoon period may be over. Following the birth of your baby you will have to learn new parenting skills, while redefining the rules and roles of your marriage relationship.

During your thirties you will begin to reassess your marriage and see if this is really how you want to live for the rest of your life. In the forties it is common for the marriage to suffer a period of turmoil as you both enter into midlife. After your children leave, you will probably find that you can put energy and life back into your marriage. You will enter into a new, fulfilling stage that may even be superior to the romance you felt in early marriage.

Your Child's Personality. The next factor in how you will parent is the personality and style of the child. Each child is an individual from the moment of birth, and carries within him or her a personality consisting of genetic factors from both parents, the experiences of development within the womb, birth, infancy, and childhood, and the place the child holds in the family.

It is important to accept your children as individuals with distinct personalities, capabilities, and needs. Getting to know each child is a challenge. Consider your children as partners in your relationship, and listen to what they can and will tell you.

From the moment of birth your children have the ability to signal their needs for care. They can guide and reward you. Some children signal more clearly than others, but whatever characteristics your children have, you will be able to enjoy them more if you watch for and listen to their cues as you explore and discover their unique personalities.

Your children's passage through the life cycle will take them on a search for trust (the foundation of their self-esteem in infancy). They will move on to independence and freedom as toddlers. As they move out into the neighborhood, they begin to develop the initiatives and creativity that will follow them through life.

During school age, children learn how to put their skills to work. Adolescence, of course, is a time of finding themselves and learning who they are (not just your version) and what they want to be in the future.

What makes up a child's personality?

GENETIC FACTORS
  Sex
  Appearance
  Intelligence
  Health

ENVIRONMENT
  Loving/hostile
  Harsh/benign
  Flexible/rigid
  Rich/poor
  Hot/cold
  Rural/urban

BIRTH ORDER
  Only
  Oldest
  Second of Two
  Middle
  Baby

WAYS OF STRIVING FOR:
  Affection
  Acceptance
  Attention

Your Family's Developmental Stage. Ultimately the developmental stage which you, your oldest child, and your family are undergoing as a single unit will define your parenting style. The key stages that most families go through are:

1. Courtship and marriage
2. First child born
3. Toddler
4. Preschool play age
5. School age
6. Adolescence
7. Launching the early adult

Each of these stages carries with it predictable stresses and problems that you as an individual, your marriage, and your family must face. Each also carries with it great opportunities to help your children develop into healthy human beings.

In the next few chapters, we will look closely at the challenges you will face during each of these stages, as well as at the actions that you can take to give your children a strong start in life.

2

MARRIAGE: THE FOUNDATION OF THE FAMILY

The first stage of the family cycle begins with courtship and continues until the birth of your first child. This stage is one of the most important, because it lays the foundation for all that follows.

This is a wonderful yet confusing period as both of you, man and woman, are emerging into your own adulthood. How you enter it depends much on how your mother and father parented you.

You are both working on major tasks as you pull up roots from your own parents and step into the adult world. Whom you chose as your mate, how you develop your own marriage, and how you resolve issues of power, independence, and sexuality will be the cornerstone of your family and determine how you will parent your children.

Courtship: How Your Choice of Mate Affects Your Marriage

Have you ever wondered, reviewing all the people you ever knew, what the magical qualities were that attracted you to your mate? And haven't you ever wondered why, out of all the people your spouse knew before you, why he or she picked you?

"Falling in love" is like two halves coming together to make a whole. Everything feels right in balance. It is that state of bliss in which both you and your partner seem to have found the perfect person who is able to cover for your deficiencies and enhance your strengths. You each appear to one another as the most charming, beautiful, handsome, intelligent, humorous, and wonderful person. Your loved one can do no wrong.

Love is as misleading as it is blissful. It is a wonderful state of harmony. If someone points out a deficiency you instantly are angry that anyone could attack such a wonderful person. Your lover seems to appreciate your qualities as no one else has before, and you feel that this is the one person who sees and accepts you as you really are. No one else has ever understood and appreciated you as well as this person.

However, in all families this state of bliss only covers potential stress factors that usually do not come into existence until after the honeymoon. During courtship both partners, following nature's survival plan, are unconsciously hiding their vulnerabilities from the person they most wish to win over.

No one knows better than you the areas of vulnerability in your own family. You, like most young adults, probably looked at the problems of your own parents and vowed fervently not to repeat them. With this knowledge you probably tried to eliminate the traits, hoping that the destructive messages you received from your own parents would not surface again in your life.

These traits, however, are not disposed of as you hoped. They are secreted in hidden places, waiting to surface later. Not only do you hope that you will not repeat the problem, but you actively search out a mate who seems to have the qualities which would rescue you from your parents' misery and make you a whole person. Unfortunately, in this quest, your hidden insecurities may well be matched by the just as well hidden insecurities of the person to whom you were attracted.

Couples seem to fall in love with people who have the same kind, level, and intensity of insecurity and conflict. You probably fell in love with a person who not only had the same kind of problems, but had them at the same level and intensity. That is the mysterious, "chemical" attraction that people have for one another: the sharing of the same basic insecurities.

The real attraction, however, is not only the sharing of vulnerabilities but the magical attraction of how your chosen one has developed new and different ways of coping with the same old problem. This means to you that the person understands you as no one ever has before, and offers to share with you his or her unique way of coping. Well, you think, your old ways didn't work too well; maybe this knight in shining armor (or damsel in the tower) is going to come and rescue you from old dragons and whisk you off to live happily ever after. It is as if you were two persons, each wearing smiling masks, carved out of all the ingenious strategies you have developed to conquer your vulnerabilities.

And so you view each other not as you really are, but masked as the person you wish the other to see—a wonderfully competent, strong, and attractive individual. Unfortunately, lurking behind each of your painted disguises are the dark, true shadows you had hoped to escape. If your parents passed on healthy messages about how to deal with your vulnerabilities, your chances are much better for choosing a spouse who received equally healthy messages. And you will in all probability pass these on to your children. If, however, you do possess unhealthy and conflicting messages, you will in all probability be attracted to a person who contains similar perspectives.

It becomes easy to understand how two kind, gentle, well-meaning people carry within them two conflicting messages that can doom them to a lifetime of struggle over any or all of the stresses they will surely face. Who, however, ever checks out these essential factors when madly in love and showing only his or her best face during courtship?

What does this mean to you, your marriage, and your future family? It means that you can enhance your chances for success if you understand the strengths and weaknesses of both yourself and your partner and learn from one another. By learning to know yourself you learn to know your partner; and by knowing your partner you come to know yourself.

Marriage: Learning to Live Together

Early marriage is the time to find out how much you care about each other, to clarify expectations, and to settle misunderstandings. It's easier to talk about things that are wrong. The turning point of the honeymoon is when you take your relationship out of fantasies of and perfection and begin to accept each other in reality.

The major task you and your spouse must accomplish is to learn to live together as a unique couple rather than as the kind of family you grew up in. This is the time that you as a couple can explore the similarities and differences between your families' values, goals, expectations and needs. You can negotiate a workable level in which you both can learn from each other, and share in new ways of doing old things and old ways of doing new things. A strong personal identity for both you and your partner is the key. That means being able to make choices based on self-knowledge rather than out-of-control compulsion.

This includes assuming new roles and relationships as a couple, relative to your siblings, your parents, your friends, your work.

You have to sort through priorities and establish new rules. You probably think you are working on such petty issues as who puts the toothpaste cap back on, or which way to put in the toilet paper, or who does the dishes and who takes out the trash. These issues really revolve around the old bugaboos of power, independence, and self-esteem. These are the concerns around which you will set patterns that will become part of your family's personality and style: how you handle disagreements, anger, approval, disappointment, and affection.

You will also be establishing a pattern of who is in control, when each partner is in control, and how power is handled in your family. It is during this stage that you are setting up your communication patterns, your power dynamics, and rules and regulations in your family. Your disagreements and fights are useful at this stage, for it is through constructive resolution of conflict that you will grow. If, however, your conflicts end in loss of self-esteem and senseless power struggles, your family may become an arena for warfare.

Your goals during this period are to learn to function as a couple, rather than as individuals; to negotiate new boundaries; to sort your priorities in relationships; and to establish new rules that are mutually satisfying to both of you. The major issues you will face are how to deal with conflict, how to express and control feelings, and how to regulate your way of relating to the outside world. You will be setting patterns that can make or break your marriage.

Failure at this stage is often due to unrealistic myths of an ideal relationship. Failure can also come from continuing dependence on your own family of origin. You will experience signs of difficulties in your relationship if differences in your styles of communication and negotiation become destructive and nonproductive.

In a healthy marriage partners realize they can benefit from having the same problems because they understand each other in a way no one else can and learn different coping strategies from one another.

How Differences Can Affect Your Relationship

If you, as a couple, cannot recognize the similarities in your problems, you may torment each other, trying to force your partner to solve the problems that you both have.

Although you chose your partner because you believed that he or she was different from you, you look to your partner's coping strategies to save you and make yourself whole. You want to be more like your partner, but once the honeymoon is over, many people are surprised and concerned when they realize the partner is more alike than different. Many partners spend the next twenty years trying to change each other.

If your marriage falls victim to wanting to change each other and emphasizing each other's imperfections, you can spend the rest of your lives torturing and blaming. It is a no-win situation, and not only do the marriage partners lose, but so does the rest of the family. If, on the other hand, when each partner has a good sense of his or her identity and is open to learn from the other, the partners do have the potential to become more of their dream of a whole person. They "fit" together and make each other whole because, although their basic insecurities are the same, their styles of coping with life are different.

The self-assured attracts the meek, the practical attracts the fun-loving, the passive attracts the aggressive, the leader attracts the follower. When it works, the system is one of learning and growth. The slob learns to be a bit neater while the cleanliness zealot becomes less compulsive; the spender becomes more responsible and the worrier panics less; the angry one grows less volatile as the restrained one becomes more assertive; the workhorse relaxes and has more fun at the same time the care-free partner becomes more organized. There is potential for positive growth for each as partners give each other the space to change, expand and grow.

Dependence. If you have basic insecurities dealing with dependence, you will probably be attracted to a person who has those same insecurities.

Lisa was a shy, retiring woman who was thrilled when she married Jack, a defiant freethinker. She believed Jack could save her from a dull future. During their courtship she reveled in his daring, risk-taking behavior, and he appreciated her quiet subservience. After marriage, however, Lisa began to resent his high-wheeling business efforts and began to nag him to change, to get a regular job, to settle down. She forgot the qualities for which she married him and wanted him to become, in fact, more like her.

Sexuality. Ardith was a cool, elegant beauty who shared a mutual attraction with Tom, a wildly flamboyant, sexually exuberant man. It was a match made in heaven, each person thinking they would save each other; Ardith would bring elegance and refinement to Tom, Tom would bring flamboyance and life to Ardith. After their first child, Ardith and Tom went in for counseling. It became clear that basic sexual insecurity formed their basic attraction. Their different way of coping with it was their undoing. Tom thought Ardith frigid, passionless, and too attached to the baby. Ardith accused Tom of being oversexed, unfaithful, and a poor father to the baby.

Self-Esteem. When first married, Kitty and Jeff, both successful professionals, had an excellent marriage. They were compatible in every way and had seemed to easily resolve their power and independence conflicts. Then they began their family, and Kitty quit her job to keep the home fires burning. Kitty was a person who spent money freely and carelessly, and as long as she was bringing in money, there was no problem. Jeff, however, was accustomed to spending very cautiously. Kitty coped with her insecurities by spending money freely; it made her feel good about herself. Jeff coped with his insecurities by self-denial. Without the double paycheck their relationship suffered from blaming and trying to change each other.

Power. John, a quiet and intense engineer, was the first child and oldest brother to three sisters. He was accustomed to power and using it indiscriminately. He was attracted to and married Blanche, who was the second child with an older brother. John was attracted by Blanche's submissiveness, as she was by his aggressiveness. During their first months of marriage, she rarely questioned him openly and seemed subservient, while resenting her role. As children came into the family, Blanche found she could use them indirectly to express her hostility toward John.

Healthy Marriages

A healthy marriage is one in which the partners have come to grips with their insecurities. They have come to share power and have developed trust, commitment, and intimacy. The man and woman both have a relationship that enhances their self-esteem. In that relationship sexuality gives pleasure to both partners, and intimacy allows both partners freedom while giving them each a sense of belonging.

The more mature and self-aware the partners are during

courtship, the more able they are to choose a partner who truly fits and makes a mutual whole. Mature people are more aware of who they are and why they do things. They make choices based on information and knowledge rather than on blind emotions based on old family patterns. They are less likely to develop a mask that is contrary to their true personality, that hides and covers insecurities. They are also less likely to be fooled by others' masks.

A healthy marriage involves feelings of love, sharing, caring and commitment. Partners in a healthy marriage use conflict as a tool for learning and growing. Flexible roles in a healthy marriage allow both marriage partners to be unique, while at the same time providing a wholeness and trust in the relationship. A basic sensitivity to needs and mutual respect gives both partners a sense of importance and high self-esteem. Rules and regulations in this marriage are open, clear, and concise. Both the woman and the man work out a mutually acceptable basis for how power is shared in this family. Problems are faced early, and instead of blaming one another, both partners acknowledge that mistakes are human and common and something to be solved or negotiated. Most of all, healthy marriages are full of joy, fun, forgiveness, and appreciation.

Patterns to Avoid in Marriage

Most couples marry with the desire to love, honor, and respect the partner. Most married people want their marriage to be successful and to bring happiness. Most marriages begin with the expectation that they will bring out the best in two individuals.

What happens along the way? What are the patterns with which your own parents lived? What are the ones to avoid? An ounce of prevention is worth a pound of cure—and that means the earlier you can discern problem patterns cropping up, and the earlier you can stop them, the better chance you have for your "dream" marriage.

Unhealthy marriage patterns are those that include no conflict and no feeling. There are rigid roles which do not allow for the partners to become unique individuals in their own rights. The communication patterns are unclear and fuzzy. Because of a basic insensitivity and lack of respect, neither party has much self-esteem. Unhealthy marriages are joyless, lifeless, and destructive.

"Perfect" Marriages

Some marriages look perfect to outsiders because the couple always agree with each other and never quarrel. Although this may appear perfect, it is, in reality, a relationship that is shallow and detrimental. When there is no conflict there is no chance for growth and development in the relationship.

In some enmeshed relationships, the couple are so afraid of rocking the boat that they agree to retreat from all problems and live together in peace—at any price. The price they will pay, of course, is their individuality and their uniqueness as human beings. While such a marriage may appear perfect to outsiders, there is usually one partner who is not in full agreement with the peace-at-any-price tag and hides feelings of anger and hostility. But this spouse is afraid to say so, hides his or her emotions and complaints, and feels trapped in a prison of quiet desperation.

When partners are afraid of dissension, and the couple are afraid of losing each other's trust and love, a fragile relationship is created, one that can break from stress at any time. When children come along, the fires are already smoldering, and many times the children then become the innocent victims of these hidden stresses.

Constant Warfare

Just as destructive are couples who do not know how to express love and affection and spend a lifetime of getting close by fighting. Every word, action, and occurrence is a reason to fight. It becomes a game, and the name of the game is Win/Lose: I win, you lose. There is no in-between ground. Great energy goes into making the other person a loser—at the expense of the marriage. Many times the fights may hide an inability to experience an intimate relationship. The trouble with the warring couple is that such painful and destructive things are said and done that often this marriage cannot be put together again.

Disengaged Marriages

Partners who go each their own way—"You do your thing and I'll do mine, and maybe we'll meet along the way"—are just as false and shallow. Many times they have not reached the level of maturity where each is able to share a mutual intimacy, and therefore they use the marriage as a false front for society. Disengaged marriages are perpetual Peter Pan and Wendy combinations; the partners are unable to grow up to give comfort and love as adults. The couple can't work out power divisions or rules, and so there is a dangerous vacuum if children do come.

Their communication patterns are fuzzy and unclear because neither partner wants to commit himself or herself. There is no conflict, but also no feelings and, of course, little sense of wholeness and of belonging.

A Word of Advice

When you talk with people who have been married twenty years or more, they will confide that it's important to remember that there is no such thing as a perfect marriage. All of us can recognize some destructive patterns cropping up at some times in our marriage. Most of us have marriages that slide up and down on the health continuum somewhere throughout the life cycle of the family. Sometimes our marriages are better than others, sometimes they are not so hot. Sometimes just toughing it out through difficult times until the next stage is what it takes to get a shaky marriage back on its feet.

It is unrealistic to think that your marriage is going to be peaches and cream during your whole family cycle. There are going to be ups and downs. Pain is part of life, and people who think that they can live a painless life by buying a painkiller in the local drugstore or can have a painless marriage by just following some simple rules will be faced with disappointment.

Because divorce is so painful for children of all ages, it is especially important that parents strive to avoid the patterns that lead to divorce and, if they get themselves caught in destructive patterns, do everything in their power to get out of them—rather than shatter their children's family security.

In-laws

To a great extent, success in your marriage will depend on how separated each of you has become from your family of origin. Research shows that people tend to recreate relationship patterns from their own family of origin and to choose a mate who has a personality similiar to a parent's in order to work out old problems in new ways.

If either you or your mate is too attached to your parents or family of origin, you cannot make the commitment that it takes for a successful marriage. If either of you is enmeshed in the family of origin, you cannot establish the identity you need as a partner in a marriage. Cutting the umbilical cord also means developing relationships and friendships outside the family. If you cannot replace your family system with a social system, you will experience tremendous loneliness that may force you into a marriage that is not right.

The most common problem young adults face is separating from the family of origin. Of course, extreme closeness and dependency are vital when children are infants, but healthy parents begin to detach during the toddler stage and complete the process when they launch their child in adulthood. This, in fact, is the basic task of parenthood: to prepare a child for adulthood.

You and your parents have to separate from each other if you are to accomplish one of the most important tasks in marriage: to make your spouse the most important person in your life. This may be more difficult if you have not yet left your parents behind emotionally. If you go into marriage and take your family of origin into it, your marriage will certainly be in trouble.

One of the challenges of early marriage is to shift your loyalty not only from your family, but also from your friends. That means your spouse comes before family and friends. A marriage partner who discusses marital problems with his or her family of origin or friends has not made this important transition.

While leaving your family behind is one of your goals, finding a place for yourself in the new family is also important. If you find yourself part of a healthy family that accepts you and enriches your marriage, you are fortunate. If you find yourself in a family which does not allow individuality, not only may you have to work your way through your partner's enmeshment, but, additionally, you may have to assure that you are not equally enmeshed into losing your own individuality.

If you find yourself in a disengaged family, you may be disappointed with the lack of affection and acceptance you get from the socially isolated family members who do not have the compassion or affection to welcome anyone into their lifeless circle.

3

FIRST CHILD BORN: THE INFANT FAMILY

The next stage in your family life is the birth of your first child. It is truly the birth of your family.

The arrival of the first child may be the most difficult crisis that your family will undergo. The tradition of the extended family was to prepare the next generation for parenthood by passing on information through live role modeling and support systems. With the decline of the extended family, those traditions have become weakened, and young couples are often completely unprepared for the stresses of a new baby. They come into parenthood with idealistic fantasies and unrealistic expectations.

New mothers often do not have the information and skills they need to nourish and nurture a new baby with ease and joy. The father also often does not have the information and skills to emotionally support and care for the mother and baby. And in most cases neither parent has the support system needed to provide comfort in his or her role.

New parents need physical, emotional, and spiritual support. When they are miles away from family and friends, they often have to look to their physicians or nurse practitioners for this support. Unfortunately, these professionals are not always inclined or equipped to give new parents what they need. As a result, we have seen a rise of "how-to" books that new parents swallow up hungrily.

Information in books is not enough, though. As new parents

you need support and nurturing for yourselves. It is important that during these infant years you seek all the help and assistance your parents, relatives, siblings, friends, and community can give, without reservation or guilt.

Having a baby forever alters the patterns of your courtship and early marriage. *Your marriage will never be the same!* This change is often so shocking that many marriages suffer irreparable damage. The overwhelming majority of couples say that they went through an extensive or severe crisis when they had their first child. Parenthood is a major life change in which positions shift, and values change.

Early Crises

The first crisis parents face with their newborn is how to balance their own needs with the needs of the baby. For the first time, you may have to make sacrifices of time, money, and attention. You will feel new pressure in your marriage.

Several studies have shown a major decrease in satisfaction in the marriage after the birth of a baby. The quality of the relationship between husband and wife diminishes with the first child, and it declines steadily throughout the active parenting years. Since satisfaction in parenting is directly related to satisfaction within the marriage, it's especially important to nurture your marriage as well as your baby.

Research shows that couples who share in the pregnancy, take childbirth classes together, plan the baby's arrival in the house, put the nursery together, and read books on parenthood are able to make the transition to parenthood with less stress and strain than parents who are not facing this new pressure together.

Vulnerability to Divorce

About half of all marriages end in divorce as of 1983. The majority of these divorces were by couples between the ages of twenty-five and thirty-nine. Fifty-six percent of divorcing cou-

ples have one or two children. Divorce statistics peak among
the newly married, and there is statistical evidence that couples
who have been married between fifteen and twenty years may
be the second highest risk group. Trends show that divorce
threatens when children are very young, and again when children are in adolescence. Married couples with a new baby are
more vulnerable to divorce than any other group. The older a
man and woman are when they marry, the better the chances
that the marriage will last. Also, the longer a couple are married
before having children, the greater their chances for a successful
marriage. Couples who marry and have children early have a
poorer chance for success.

Parents' Life Cycle

While your baby is growing, you, as an individual, are going
through your own life-stage development. If you are between
twenty-two and twenty-eight, this is a period when you as a
young adult try to get into the established adult world and
seperate from your own family. If you don't do so, you can
expect to have marital problems.

Having a baby doesn't solve marital problems. The necessity
of relating to the baby not only exaggerates the parents' marital
problems but brings up unresolved conflicts each has with his
or her own parents. The relationship is sure to suffer when a
husband has not separated himself from his mother. Identifying
his wife with his mother during pregnancy is a problem because
his wife may become even more like "a mother" when she is
pregnant. It may be all right to have sex with your wife, but it's
not all right to have sex with your mother! The marriage will
be stressed as well when the wife has not separated from her
family of origin.

Healthy Family Patterns

Your new family is in a most delicate balance. Three relationships need nurturing: the mother and the child, the father
and the child, and the husband and wife. In healthy families
all three relationships are unique and strong. Should the in-

tensity of any one attachment shift, your family will be out of balance, and adjustments in relationships will quickly take place to stabilize the unbalanced family structure.

Patterns to Avoid

There are four major themes around which family problems tend to revolve: sex, dependence, self-esteem, and power.

If you as a new mother are too wrapped up in your baby and neglect your relationship with your husband, his tie to both of you weakens as your attachment to the child grows more intense. This is one way hazardous family patterns get started early in family life.

Sex and affection are frequently the first arena of conflict in the young family, and the mother and father are the most important players in this game. If the mother puts her affection into an excessively strong bond with a child, the father may look elsewhere; sexual issues may become a major problem in the family.

The second theme that rises in the new family is dependence. As the baby is completely dependent on the mother, so the mother may find herself completely dependent on the father. This will make self-esteem an important issue in the relationship between the mother and father.

Finally, there are roles that have to be assumed and power issues that have to be resolved. Who is making the rules in your family? How are they being made? Is it a shared or a one-sided affair? How is the power shared? These themes will constantly be played throughout the life of your family.

With the first baby, many couples find that the romance of the honeymoon fades and the relationship reaches a turning point. You may both begin to wonder if you've made a mistake. Your partner is full of flaws you never saw before. You question whether you can work things out. Sometimes the stress of a new baby starts a stage signaled by an escalating series of arguments that never seem to get resolved. You may begin to notice traits you don't like in your partner (dirty diapers in the toilet and piles of dirty clothes in the corners don't help).

If you, as a couple, can express your feelings, communicate

your concerns, and work on problem-solving and negotiating, your love may deepen as your early and unrealistic romantic love is replaced by openness and honesty.

It's hard to be perfect all the time with the twenty-four-hour-a-day task of parenting an infant. The more fully people express different facets of their personalities—good and bad—from the beginning of the relationship, the less shocking the turning point will be. The more honest you both are, the easier it is to achieve intimacy. Putting your best self forward all the time is not only a strain, it also keeps the relationship from growing.

During this phase, your relationship will grow if you express yourselves more fully, revealing hidden feelings, weaknesses, insecurities, and fears, and if you are equally willing to listen and accept what your spouse has to say about his or her true self. If, however, you avoid this process, you and your partner are forced to play uneasy roles that are only partly true. By failing to reveal your whole self you make a contract as an impostor. Taking the risk is tough for some people. You fear that you won't be loved if you are really known. But you won't be truly loved unless you are fully known.

Common Issues Confronting New Parents

For the first time in your life you may be confronted with the need to defer your own needs and desires to those of someone else. The working mother will be confronted with a completely dependent human being for twenty-four hours a day, seven days a week, four weeks a month.

New mothers may be especially disappointed in the lack of creative outlets in their lives. They report a loss of self-esteem and are confused by their changing roles. Women may be less sure of themselves as valued human beings and are more sensitive and need the support of the father as they have never needed it before.

The father will be confronted, and perhaps frightened, by the complete dependence of his wife and baby upon him. Few mothers and fathers are prepared for the total exhaustion a new baby brings to their lives.

Money may become an issue. Pregnancy and childbirth are expensive; if the mother held a job before the baby's birth, the couple may miss the extra income.

Most couples lack the understanding of the distance the new baby puts between them and how to creatively solve this issue. Both mothers and fathers may be surprised by the change in their sexuality and sex lives. The mother's sex needs may be low during the first few months, and the mother and father may both wonder if their sex life will ever be the same.

It is important that you, as a couple, use this time to explore new ways of communicating your affection and appreciation and to try new ways of giving pleasure to one another. It is important that a couple develop a support system that, in addition to each other, includes family, friends, physicians, community organizations, and even professional help (individual or family counseling) if they feel that they cannot cope by themselves.

Understanding Your Infant

Task: Developing Trust

Infants can't speak yet, but if they could, these are some of the things they would like you to know.

Your baby cares that you want to do the best for him or her, even if at times he or she seems pretty impossible. The infant is taking in everything new through all senses: skin, eyes, mouth, ears. It's through these senses that you show your love and affection and care.

As the infant gets older he or she will be able to reach out and get some of the things he or she needs, but not now. It might interest you to know that your baby was born with the desire and ability to learn. What you do with your face, voice, body, and hands gives your child his or her first experience with human relationships. The child learns through sight, sound, and touch how it feels to be loved and how to love and trust in return.

Trust. Probably one of the most important challenges of infancy is developing the capacity for trust—a trust that will endow the child with the ability to hope and dream for the rest of life. The ease with which the infant learns to trust others—and trust himself or herself—depends directly on how you care for him or her.

If a child learns to expect that his or her needs will be taken care of, the child learns to trust himself or herself, parents, and forces outside the family. If needs are not met and the child receives inconsistent, inadequate, or reluctant care, he or she will develop a sense of distrust which may carry forward for the rest of life.

A child who develops a weak sense of trust grows up impatient and unresponsive to other people, and either avoids people or constantly demands attention.

Play. One way a baby learns to trust is through the joy and wonder of play. A baby's first play object in life is his or her own body. The feel, touch, and smell of the mother's body comes next. Your touch, smile, voice, and face have special meaning, and the strong emotional bond that forms is very important. Babies not only want to be fed and touched, but love your eyes and your voice.

Play and the endless repetition of attempts to touch and hold objects help an infant learn that one's body can do one's bidding. He or she learns to expect that things which disappear, such as the mother, the bottle, and the face which plays "peek-a-boo," do return. Playing with parents is pure joy, and the fun that you have helps build the trust that the child will be able to bring to all future human relationships. The give-and-take of play provides the experiences the child needs to grow and develop and trust self and others.

If you did not respond to his or her needs, the infant probably could not learn to depend on anyone and would learn to expect nothing. The infant would lose natural spontaneity and would soon become unresponsive, listless, inactive. He or she would become a poor eater and poor sleeper and would show symptoms of failure to thrive.

During the first year the infant learns to coordinate eye and hand movements, to discriminate between flavors, smells, touches, sights, and sounds, and to eat solid foods. Your child will probably give you great delight as he or she masters simple skills such as turning over, sitting up, and standing. With your help the child can learn to achieve the emotional stability which will make life more comfortable and predictable.

Tips for Parents

After infancy, a child will probably never again be so dependent on you to meet his or her needs, so meeting the infant's needs is of critical importance. Provide your child with consistent and reliable responses as you help guide him or her through infancy. If the infant can count on you to fill his or her needs, it is easier to develop a sense of basic trust in the world. When you cuddle, fondle, play with, and talk to a baby with love and care, he or she develops a sense of the world as a safe place to be and learns to accept people as helpful and dependable.

When your baby is cold, wet, or hungry, can he or she count on you to bring comfort? When you come when your child needs you, he or she learns that you are trustworthy. From this trust the child will learn to postpone gratification, knowing the needs will be met in due time.

If you are unpredictable and unreliable and are not there when your baby needs you, he or she may develop a sense of mistrust that will haunt him throughout life. The child may carry forward a basic fear and suspicion toward the world in general and people in particular. If the child experiences consistent abuse, neglect, and lack of love, the results may be devastating.

Actions That Encourage Trust— and Actions That Promote Distrust

TRUST	DISTRUST
Bonding at birth	No bonding
Responding to needs	Ignoring needs
Loving your baby	Physical abuse
Touching	Emotional abuse
Positive reinforcement	Negative reinforcement
Playing	Cleaning only
Sensory stimulation— touch, sight, hearing, tasting, smelling	Lack of stimulation or excessive stimulation
Leaving and returning	Sneaking out
Picking up when crying	Letting cry alone
Soothing	Non-soothing
Comforting	Non-comforting
Flexible schedules	Rigid schedules
Meeting basic needs	Avoidance
Feeding	Not feeding
Cleaning diapers	Leaving dirty
Trusting self	Outside pressure
Breastfeeding, or bottle feeding with cuddling, closeness	Sticking a bottle in mouth uncaringly
Marriage intact	Marriage in trouble

4

THE TODDLER FAMILY

As your children progress from infancy to toddler age—ages two and three—a wonderful thing is happening: They change from more or less passive babies for whom you do things to active and fiercely independent human beings. At two a child begins to test your new efforts to set limits and share power. New issues may determine when and how and why you fight, and with emotions running high, you will have to negotiate how and when feelings of affection and anger will be expressed.

Transition Crises

Your infant probably becomes a toddler at a time when you are grappling with the questions about what it means to be an adult. You may be examining the essential problems and satisfactions of your life. You may be thinking about your sources of disappointment and grief.

Both parents may be in the process of working to become established and accepted in their careers. Both may feel more comfortable in the role as spouse, but toddlers add to the complexity of married life.

You probably are feeling increased financial demands. You may still be trying to get your parents to regard you as equals rather than children. Fortunately, at this stage you and your spouse probably have a lot of energy, capabilities, and potential to deal with external and internal pressures.

Common Issues Confronting Toddler Parents

The most common issues that confront most parents of toddlers are time, letting go, setting limits, and toilet training. Most parents talk about the difficulty of giving a child the extra special time she or he needs. How do you find time for yourself, your partner, your baby, and your jobs? How do you keep open communications about sexuality? You may be facing intense fights as your child begins to assert his or her independence, and you find for the first time that you and your spouse have different ideas about discipline.

In the meantime you are coping with the problems of letting go while needing to set limits. This can be a delicate balance, because there are real dangers out there.

Toilet training either becomes a battle royal fraught with shame and doubt which will persist throughout the lifetime of your child or a process which helps your child develop independence and self-esteem.

Because of your toddler's changing needs, you may find yourself tested more and angry more than you expected. It may be difficult to handle that anger and not turn it against your child, your mate, or even yourself. It may be a blow to your self-esteem if you personalize the "no's" and "I hate you's" your toddler begins to say. You may find that your child's rebellion brings out your own hang-ups as you recognize yourself in him or her, and try to fight it.

Healthy Family Patterns

At this stage you should be working openly to develop a sense of wholeness as a family while still keeping your individuality by not becoming smothered as a mother or a father. Your toddler should also be allowed to be an individual in his or her own right.

Because living with young children is so hard on a marriage, both partners must work to maintain open communications. Lovemaking may take on new meanings as you both learn to be tender and compassionate. Exhaustion takes a toll in your life, and it is important that you both work to solve resulting problems in a way that is mutually productive.

Thus, healthy families will be more flexible in their roles at this time, and for the benefit of the child and the family, the father will want to share in caretaking tasks.

The most important relationship in the healthy family is the parents' relationship. Healthy coalitions are established when parents support each other regarding the children, children support one another, and grandparents (or in-laws) support the family as a unit, and when the children know that they can't play one parent against the other.

In a healthy family, parents will share in leadership. When they disagree, they use it as an experience to work things out without bringing the child into it. Each parent respects the other's right to discipline and guide the child.

Family Patterns to Avoid

Disengaged Families. If you as parents have not resolved basic conflicts, your baby may become a helpless victim. The most destructive pattern that may accompany a new family is when the mother weakens her bond to the father as she develops strong impermeable bonds with her toddler. The father is out in the cold, and the child is put in an impossible position in a triangle in which everyone stands to lose.

From this basic position there are many ways to play the game. The parents may remain together physically, but be emotionally estranged, and the family becomes disengaged. The disengaged family cannot provide the nurturing and basic support the child needs to thrive. Children of parents who are at war either passively or aggressively may be used as weapons by the parents. Or they may be ignored in the battle and left to fend for themselves.

When the children are used as the weapons of war between

their parents, the parents place the child in one end of the triangle and wage their personal wars through this innocent victim. The wars may be over money, discipline, or some other major issue. All triangles are destructive to children and to the family. Because this is too heavy a role for any person, let alone a child, to handle, sooner or later the grief that is brought upon the child will come to the forefront in various compensating behaviors.

For instance, when a toddler is engaged in a triangle, where the issues the parents do battle over are discipline, letting go, and toilet training, independence and toilet training often become the focus of the child. She or he may become ill-behaved, impossible to toilet-train, and because of this behavior, make it impossible for the parents to leave home.

The parents' reaction may cause insecurity and low self-esteem in the toddler. This may in turn retard his or her development physically, intellectually, and socially.

When children join against parents, when one parent joins against the other parent through the grandparents, when grandparents side with a child against parents or with one parent against the other, enormous trouble will arise in the family.

Enmeshed Families. When two insecure parents build a relationship based only on their weaknesses, they may cling together and depend on one another in a way which surrenders their separate identities. When they have children, the children are included in this relationship; neither parent is willing to complain or face sources of trouble, and neither are the children. Children who grow up to be dependent and insecure cannot discover their own identities, and the "closeness" of their families disguises weakness and tyranny.

Problems in enmeshed families may erupt into divorce during the toddler stage, but more often they are hidden in established patterns that will develop into major conflicts in the coming years and emerge full-blown when the children reach adolescence. Year after year the unacknowledged grievances and dangerous patterns harden.

Children become deeply saturated with family traits until the pattern is almost in their blood, to be passed on from one generation to the next—unless the family is able to break out of the pattern. The earlier the family members face their insecurities, the easier it will be to work them out.

Understanding Your Toddler

Task: Developing Independence; Eliminating Shame and Doubt

Toddlers need to hold on when they want to and push away when they need to. They are engaged in a search for independence built on new dimensions of motor and mental development.

Physical and Intellectual Growth. During the second and third year, children learn how to stand on their own two feet and begin to explore the world on their own. They will probably insist on feeding themselves, even if—especially if—it means making a mess. Language, too, gives them a new independence and sense of self. They may drive you crazy repeating new words: "me" and "mine." Most of all, they express again and again their sense of freedom and independence in a single word, "no," which seems to get a great rise out of you. Strong and insistent "no's" (and temper tantrums) may seem to defy all external control. However, this period will soon be over, and it is vital to developing self-reliance.

Imagine how exciting it is to a child to become aware of himself as a separate individual who can act independently of you through doing things on his own as his nerves and muscles mature.

Imagine your child's delight in holding on to or dropping things at will; learning to walk, to talk, to take, and to give; and, beginning to learn how to control muscles for urination and defecation.

Social Growth. During this stage it is important that toddlers learn to separate themselves as individuals as they walk, climb, open and close, drop, push and pull, hold on and let go. They take great pride in all these new accomplishments and want to do everything themselves. Independence does have its limits, however.

For the first time toddlers begin to doubt themselves as they look at others watching them, and begin to adjust their views to those who judge them. Adjusting to toilet training and other social demands contributes to a sense of independence. At the same time, though, with too much judgment, they may develop a lasting sense of shame and doubt.

Psychological Growth. In discovering the pleasure of holding and releasing feces and urine at will, toddlers learn there is a right way and a wrong way to release what they regard as possessions. They can lose face and suffer shame by displeasing you; or, by releasing their feces at the right time, in the right place, they can get lavish praise and warm approval. Thus some psychologists believe that the type of toilet training you give can affect a child's personality development. If the training is too strict or too permissive, they say, the child will develop future problems ranging from obsessive neatness to destructive messiness.

Play. A toddler soon learns what looks right and what does not look right in your eyes. This newfound perception adds to his pleasure in exerting his will.

The pleasant experience of learning to assert independence is usually accompanied by the unpleasant discovery of limits to how, when, and where he may eat, walk, play, or defecate. When you allow him choices—for example, if you don't force him to play with the ball if he wants the blocks—you give him some sense of the boundaries of self-determination.

In toddlers, a healthy sense of independence is shown by freedom and confidence in independent actions and choices. It is balanced by self-control in cooperating with others (learning to share a stuffed animal with a playmate) and the ability to use help and guidance (seeing how to beat the drum). A weak sense of autonomy is shown by doubt, indecision, shame, exaggerated help-seeking, exaggerated refusal of needed help, or exaggerated forms of self-assertion such as defiance.

Tips on Parenting

During this second and third year, your toddler needs a great deal of patient, mature, and loving care. If you can recognize and accept his need to do what he can do at his own pace and in his own time, he can develop the feeling that he can control his impulses, himself, and his environment.

As he reaches the peak of willfulness, it may be the time that you have to teach him to behave in socially proper ways. Toilet training will probably be the most important issue facing you. Although he may resist training for some time, he will eventually submit to it. It may seem that in the battle of the toilet bowl there is a battle of wills. You will probably decide sooner or later that he cannot say no to every single request, and that he will have to learn to live in society and respect your wishes. Your child will benefit if you gently try to help him learn social behavior without crushing his will.

If you are insensitive to his needs for independence and freedom, and shame him excessively when he has a bowel accident, or if you are impatient and do for him what he is capable of doing himself, you pass on shame and doubt. If you are consistently overprotective or criticize too harshly, you are creating doubt about his own abilities to control his world and himself.

If a child leaves this stage with less independence than shame or doubt, he may be handicapped in future attempts toward self-determination. As a consequence, he may have trouble learning basic skills, and want to hide inadequacies. But he will be well prepared to be independent at later phases if you can guide him with love, patience, and understanding.

Actions That Enhance Independence— and Actions That Promote Guilt

INDEPENDENCE	GUILT
Letting go	Holding on
Saying no with discretion	Saying no all the time
Playing with child	Hitting child
Giving praise	Saying "Shame on you"
Allowing errors	Making child feel guilty about mistakes
Letting child figure things out alone	Figuring things out for child
Letting child play with household items	Grabbing things from child
Enjoying child	Ignoring child
Realistic expectations	Unrealistic expectations
Staying positive	Losing temper
Not personalizing	Personalizing
Letting anger out in positive way	Holding anger in or taking it out on child
Not comparing child to others	Comparing child to others
Letting go, giving freedom	Letting go too much
Setting reasonable limits	Setting rigid limits

5

THE PLAY-AGE FAMILY

Once your first child has struggled through toddlerhood you are probably in for a calmer period. Your child has mastered many of the skills that were so frustrating for him or her during the toddler stage, and now goes out to explore the neighborhood.

Children in the play age—ages four and five—suddenly become social beings with social needs. They need to meet and play with others. This is the time for moving ahead. Your children now have a new sense of initiative as they make plans, set goals, and persevere in attaining them. Their behavior takes on a goal-directed, competitive, and imaginative quality. Whether they leave this stage with a sense of creativity and initiative or not depends to a considerable extent on how you respond to the child's self-initiated activities.

Transition Crises

You and your spouse are probably beginning to feel more confident in your role as adults—after all, you have probably weathered toilet training and are beginning to feel somewhat in control of your own lives. You may still be working to establish a firm, safe structure for your family's future by making strong commitments to your career, but you are still shaping your dreams, and having visions of your own possibilities in the world. You also may be torn by an opposite urge to explore and experiment.

Money may be scarce, especially if the wife is not working. If you have bought a house, the commitment of a large mortgage may be pressing. The laundry and housework may seem overwhelming, especially if you have another baby at this time.

Common Issues Confronting Play-Age Parents

Although this is a joyous time to see your child reaching out, there are three new issues you will probably face. As your child goes out in the neighborhood and brings friends and neighbors back to your home, you will probably encounter for the first time unsolicited judgment on your parenting skills. Your housekeeping skills and even your life suddenly seem open to criticism as your child reveals everything that you have kept private over the years. You will also be faced with the dilemma of letting your child explore the neighborhood while setting the boundaries of that neighborhood. If you have another child, you may experience sibling rivalry. You may find that with the birth of another child your play-age child has regressed to thumb-sucking, bed-wetting, drinking out of the baby bottle, wanting to breast-feed and behaving like the baby who has usurped his kingdom.

You will struggle to give clear messages at a level your child can understand. As you begin to see that your child is quite a different person from yourself you must allow him or her that difference.

Setting limits with built-in consequences for your child and then allowing him to accept the consequences of his actions may be a difficult task.

As your child experiments, it's important that you not let yourself build up too much guilt. Try not to compare him or her to other kids. At the same time, give the play-age child more attention than you give a newly arrived baby.

A major problem for parents at this stage is finding time for themselves and finding time for keeping their marriage together.

It takes special attention to build fun into your lives: fun in your personal life, fun in your marriage, and fun in parenting.

If you are both working, it is especially important that you find good baby-sitters and child care. For the sake of your marriage it is important that both parents share the work load. If the mother has been a wage earner before the birth and has left her job, finances are probably a large problem in the marriage. In a growing family it is not unusual for the marriage to be affected by changing roles: who works outside the house, who stays home, who empties the garbage, who has power. Communications in sexuality and sex are especially important. Sexual difficulties are often avoided by giving each other comfort and pleasure without undue emphasis on intercourse.

Understanding Your Play-Age Child

Task: Developing Initiative and Eliminating Guilt

All of your past efforts will pay off as your toddler begins playing with other four- and five-year olds. You will probably find many delights as he or she shows everyone what a great job you did. On the other hand you should be prepared for your child to indiscriminately tell everyone everything.

With a growing ability to make plans, set goals, and work hard at attaining them, children discover new and wonderful uses for their imagination as they play alone and with others. At the same time a new sense of competitiveness is arising in the child—to be especially sharpened if the child must greet a new brother or sister who threatens to take over his or her special place with you.

Physical and Intellectual Growth. The four- and five-year-old is delighted to be the master of his or her own body. For example, play-age children can hold pencils and draw pictures. They can learn to ride a tricycle, run, kick a ball, and start actions without imitating others. Their language and fantasy activities are also more under control.

Play-age children are also learning about sex differences and developing more accurate understanding of their bodies. You may be dismayed by some of what the child learns through exploration and play. This is the time when the child discovers that mud can be fun!

Psychological Growth. This is an explosive time for your child. Eager to learn, the child finds ways of channeling all his or her energies and ambitions into creative projects. Nothing seems too great for the child's daring initiative. The capes of Superman and Superwoman are vital wardrobe items. Crisis looms, though, when the child realizes that the biggest plans (a space vehicle to Mars) and fondest hopes (to fly) are doomed to failure.

A child at this stage is learning to internalize feelings and beginning to develop a conscience. This is vital to the child's personality since it will help him or her learn to keep dangerous impulses and fantasies in check for the rest of life. Forever after, the child's naive exuberance and daring will be offset by the self-observation, self-control, and self-punishment he or she has learned in life up to this point.

During the play age, children have an overwhelming desire to explore and enjoy. It is important that you allow your children to do this without making them feel guilty or inhibited so that they can develop their own sense of right and wrong and learn to control their own behavior.

Social Growth. Another significant thing is that at the same time play-age children are exploring, they are learning the rules and expectations of their family, neighborhood, and society in general. Equally important, they are learning about sex roles from both of you and beginning to relate emotionally to all members of the family. As the child grows older, he or she will begin to relate to other relatives and peers and adjust to guidelines about appearance, dress, and behavior without losing initiative and individuality.

Sexual Growth. This is the time when chances are that a boy is attracted to Mom and sees Dad as a rival, or a girl is attracted to Dad and views Mom as the enemy. This is all normal and part of the scheme of things. If you will handle these emotions with patience and humor (and don't personalize them), your child will soon find out that such attitudes are not acceptable.

Curiosity is an important indication of the development of sexual identity. When a boy is attracted to Mom, and it becomes evident that he cannot have her, he learns to model himself after Dad, because after all he won Mom. And a girl to whom it becomes evident she can't have Dad will turn to the expert, Mom. How Mom and Dad model their roles is very important in determining whether or not the child can go on to develop normal relationships in life.

Sexual growth is a dominant theme of play at this stage. Through play a child expresses his or her innermost thoughts and fantasies, and experiences all the frustrations which accompany them. Play revolves around experimenting with self-image and the roles of parents and others as the child imagines himself or herself in their places.

Tips on Parenting

You can help your child through this play-age stage by easing your authority and permitting him or her to participate as an "equal" on interesting projects and things that you can do together. In this way you help encourage spontaneity while at the same time teaching how to set and achieve goals. A child who has successfully met the challenges of this stage develops a lively imagination and is not afraid to test reality. He or she will imitate adults and anticipate and try on new roles; that's why children love dressing up and play-acting "Mommy and Daddy." Thwarted at this stage, a child will not be able to develop such spontaneity and may be suspicious and evasive and suffer from role inhibition later on.

How your child acquires initiative and creativity is dependent to a great extent on how you, as parents, respond to the activities that he or she invents. You can reinforce initiative by giving freedom and the opportunity for activities such as running, biking, sliding, skating, tussling, and wrestling. You can also reinforce initiative by encouraging fantasy and play activity, and by patiently answering the millions of questions asked each day. If you make fun of play-age children and make them feel that their motor skills are poor, that their questions are a nuisance, and that their play is silly and stupid, then they may develop a sense of guilt over self-motivated activities.

Actions That Encourage Initiative and Freedom — and Actions That Promote Guilt

INITIATIVE	GUILT
Allowing simple tasks	Doing all for child
Praising accomplishments	Criticizing child
Taking time to allow child to act independently	Being impatient
Showing affection	Showing disappointment
Allowing for imperfections	Expecting perfection
Teaching simple tasks	Ridiculing child
Letting child dress self	Dressing child
Encouraging imaginative play	Disallowing or discounting fantasy
Allowing expression of fear	Ridiculing fear
Giving honest answers about sexuality	Making child feel embarrassed
Allowing initiative	Being rigid
Giving child choices	Making child do things your way
Letting go of child	Holding on to "baby"
Trusting child's biological time clock	Trying to mold child
Working and playing with child	Criticizing work and accomplishments
Kissing, cuddling, touching, and showing affection	Not showing affection

Giving clear messages	Sending mixed messages
Allowing child to make decisions	Making all decisions
Allowing child to live with consequences	Not allowing or covering up mistakes
Offering small choices	Overwhelming child with choices
Providing positive reinforcement	Hitting or slapping
Allowing child to pick own friends	Controlling child's friends
Respecting child's feelings	Ignoring child's feelings

6

THE SCHOOL-AGE FAMILY

When your first child enters school, you pass into a stage of your family development that lasts until your child reaches puberty. For you, the parents, this will probably be a time of adjustment as your child is beginning to leave the family to create his or her own personal identity.

School-age children are no longer in the house full-time and you are no longer their sole guide. During this stage it may be a shock to find that you are vulnerable to judgment and feedback from the school and the neighborhood.

For your child, this is a time of blossoming. She or he has mastered some basic skills, begins to make some wonderful intellectual leaps. The child learns to read, to write, and to master mathematics. Your child now uses his or her earlier experience in social interaction and is able to get along with and enjoy others. During this period your child is especially comfortable in relationships with children of the same sex. This is the age when your child, with the help of schools, clubs, and friends, explores the importance of industriousness. He or she will experience the heady feeling of setting a task and succeeding in achieving goals.

Basic Issues

Until now you have been involved in giving your child most of the nurturing and guidance he or she has received. Now during the early school years, children must reach out and experience their first tastes of freedom. There will be a considerable amount of role redefinement as some parents find that letting go of their children is a wrenching experience fraught with anxiety. Research shows that fathers, even more than mothers, experience stress as their first child goes off to school.

Now, you must look at your school-age child as an individual, not an extension of yourself. And you, the mother and father, must look to yourselves as individuals rather than an extension of your child. Both of you will need to review and renew your own individuality, your marriage, your role as parent, your role as a professional. If she hasn't yet returned to an outside job or career, Mom may go back to work and become part of the breadwinning partnership. Dad may have to readjust his thinking and chip in with more household responsibilities. Even if Mom doesn't go back to a career, she may have other children (her second or third), and she will need more support and help than ever before.

How well you, the couple, communicate and renegotiate your boundaries is critical if your family is to continue to thrive. As your children become more capable and independent, you will give them their own space and allow them friends of their own.

If you are employed, or have a profession within your home, you have probably established yourself in your career. You now begin to look beyond career and marriage into your own personal development. You begin to ask what you want of this life, rather than what you should do professionally. Gail Sheehy calls this the "Catch 30 couple crises": the need for change. Couples need to change together as they both move toward personal growth and development. Instead, some couples change separately, and grow apart from the marriage and the family.

Healthy School-Age Families

Boundaries in healthy families are renegotiated as your children move out into the world.

You, as parents, have to reaffirm your marriage so that as your children enter the world on their own, they have the security of a stable family to rely on. Stretch the boundaries to allow for the children's freedom and exploration while still giving them the security and sense of wholeness they need to flower.

Healthy families are able to use the issues and problems of this stage to grow as they pass on lessons of problem-solving and negotiation to their children. Healthy parents have realistic expectations of their school-age children as they experiment and learn. Parents allow children to experience success without expecting them to think and act like adults. Healthy families are able to look at the old regulations in new ways, while at the same time considering new rules and requirements in old ways. The healthy school-age family has fun and traditions in which the family members all have an important role and place.

Patterns to Be Avoided

When parents try to change and develop through their children rather than independently on their own, both they and the children suffer. When you confuse your own needs for growth and development and put your own unrealized dreams onto your children (as by pushing them into Little League, piano, football), you are denying your children the right to be themselves, and you your right to be yourself.

There are two major dangers for the school-age family. One is the danger of becoming too rigid and not giving the child the feeling of support and belonging. Such a family does not have a sense of unity or wholeness. Each member (including the mother and the father) is so busy doing his or her own thing that there is no sense of wholeness. Each family member has his or her own goals and objectives, and is excessively independent. The father of this family may be excessively involved with his work, the mother may be concerned with outside professional or social activities, and the kids may be preoccupied by school and outside activities. Since so much time is spent on outside people and activities, meals and family activities receive low priority. Close relationships within the family do not exist. To the extent that the family is disengaged, there is no feeling of trust or intimacy, communication patterns are kept at the impersonal level, and true feelings and concerns are not expressed.

At the other end of the continuum of troubled school-age families is the enmeshed family which spends all of its time together, and the members lose their individuality. They too are afraid to discuss feelings and problems because they may threaten their excessively close relationships. Family members speak for one another, rather than allowing family members to speak for themselves. They avoid exploring outside activities and therefore cannot become unique and independent individuals.

By the time a child who has been enmeshed in a triangle with his or her parents enters school, he or she may be socially insecure and have developed a serious behavior problem in order to give the parents something on which to focus their problems. It is not uncommon for everyone else in the family to appear healthy (especially the parents) and elect this child as the scapegoat to cover up all the family problems.

Common Issues Confronting School-Age Families

Although, as a rule, the period from age six to age eleven will probably be one of calm and stability for both you and the child, it is also the most decisive period of your child's ego growth. It is this time when your child will develop the skills needed not only to survive but to thrive as a productive and creative member of society. This is the time in which your child is concerned with how things are made, how they work, and what they do. This is the time during which your child's love for you has been resolved, and she or he is ready to move on to new relationships. Probably the greatest change you will see is your need to help support your child in school relationships.

This stage may bring up new discipline issues in which the parents have different views on homework, grades, teachers, and school pressures. It is not uncommon for parents to take their children's school grades personally and begin to blame each other if there is a difference in how the issues of school are viewed. Teachers may begin to criticize and judge you as well; your self-esteem as a parent may diminish if the news is not positive.

You may now begin to confront another phase of letting go as your child asserts his will in choosing friends. If you have a strong-willed child, you may find that the child will begin to assert his or her will and defy you at an early stage.

If you have a child with learning difficulties, you may find that you are overwhelmed by ineffective advice from schools, teachers, and friends. It is not easy to depersonalize learning problems. Since some forms of learning problems are inherited, one of the parents may have to relive the pain of his or her own school experience.

If there are other children in the family, you are sure to experience sibling rivalry as all of the children are involved in finding individuality and their own unique positions within the family.

Communications, rules, and regulations once again become major issues in the family. Clear, concise rules about how you express feelings and solve problems are essential to a healthy family. As your child becomes more capable and self-sufficient, new and realistic standards of conduct must be agreed to in a democratic way. This will encourage your child to accomplish the tasks needed in order to be an effective and productive member of society.

Understanding Your School-Age Child

Task: Developing Industry and Avoiding Failure

This may be as joyful a stage for you as it is for your child as the child discovers strengths, and uses all of his or her talents and skills to begin to create and produce. This is the time when your love allows the child to move into new social relationships. This is also the time for the child to learn what success is. The child is deeply affected by failures at this age, however.

How the child works through this age points to the direction of how he or she is going to experience the rest of life: as a winner or as a loser. The child is going to need your guidance, your support, and your wisdom to help him or her experience success, while sensing your faithful protection from too much failure.

Physical and Intellectual Growth. This is an exciting period in which the child becomes a master of playing and learning and deductive reasoning. Playing marbles, checkers, and the like, and learning how to take a turn in games, a child learns how to play by the rules.

The child begins to show effort and productivity. It is an especially enthusiastic time when the most minor of details is fascinating.

At school, the child is busy learning reading, writing, and arithmetic. Reading opens a whole new world of information, as do the basic facts of science and humanities. The child begins to distinguish between fact and fiction. Hobbies, play, and recreation become important sources of discovery and learning.

This is the time when children begin to apply themselves in learning the useful skills and tools of society. The most significant event in this process is going to school, where they learn to do meaningful work, pay attention, and persevere with diligence. Work and play with peers and sense of industry and productivity bring extra joy to a school-age child's life.

Faced with so many challenges of learning and exploring, children in this stage are in danger of feeling overwhelming inadequacy and inferiority. They will store the memories of the hurts and failures they are sure to experience in the classroom or on the playground. Without the strengths honed from previous experience and the ability to successfully resolve conflicts, they may go through life experiencing deep feelings of inferiority and failure. Now, however, other adults besides parents begin to count, and an especially compassionate teacher or relative can be of great help.

Facing the challenges of this stage successfully leads to a sense of duty and accomplishment and success in school and social activities. A healthy child can put fantasy and play into better perspective, undertake real tasks with productivity, and master the tools and work habits which he or she will need to progress into adulthood.

Failure at this stage may lead to poor work habits, and the child may avoid strong competition because he or she feels doomed to mediocrity. Feelings of inferiority may generate feelings of futility and poor school behavior, and may lead to experiments with drugs, gang behavior, and cults—just for a feeling of belonging and some success even if it's negative.

Social Development. By successfully facing the expectations of family and teachers, a child learns to enjoy producing and learning. Practicing skills with success becomes a pleasure, and the child learns to cope with frustrations and failures without developing low self-esteem. A healthy child develops a tolerance for frustration and is no longer as disappointed by things he or she cannot do. It is also important for the child to meet the expectations of peers and friends, regulate his or her own behavior, and become aware of a social conscience.

By this stage, a child begins to identify with the same-sex parent, freeing his or her energy for concentration on ever-present personal, intellectual, and social tasks. Typically, the child surrounds himself or herself with friends of the same sex. You will find the child hanging around, working, playing, and studying with friends—and nothing is more embarrassing than to be found with someone of the opposite sex.

A most amazing thing happens at this stage when play activities are turned into work. Games develop into competition and cooperation, so the child frees his imagination to perform with full attention to the techniques of the game. Interested in team sports and adept at taking on the loyalties of his or her "in group," the child finds baseball, football, soccer, slumber parties, and other group activities an important part of life.

Tips on Parenting

Although it may seem as if your child is trying to escape from home, he or she badly needs your support and guidance.

When you encourage the child to make or do practical things (whether it is airplane models, tree houses, cooking or sewing), he or she will respond. The child glows when you give praise for finishing something. If, on the other hand, you consistently see the child's efforts as making a mess or causing mischief, then you bring out feelings of inferiority.

During the elementary-school years, a child's world grows. It is a vulnerable time for your child, who is no longer dependent solely on you, but also on the actions of other adults. Schoolmates and school are highly important, and constant failures in academic efforts could reinforce a sense of inferiority. A teacher who is especially sympathetic, however, can revitalize a child's sense of industry and go a long way to compensate for feelings of inferiority at home.

Actions That Enhance Industry and Accomplishment — and Actions That Promote Feelings of Failure

INDUSTRY	FAILURE
Praising and rewarding of schoolwork	Unrealistic expectations
Encouragement	Criticism
Accepting friends	Ridiculing friends
Accepting differences	Making comparisons
Teaching values	Setting no limits
Making time for effective listening	Being too busy
Consistency	Inconsistency
Flexibility	Rigidity
Allowing child freedom	Unrealistic limits
Trusting child	Distrusting child
Letting child make own mistakes	Not allowing for mistakes
Accepting child	Making child feel guilty
Encouraging outside activity	Pointing out faults
Giving responsibilty at home	Doing everything for child

Realistic expectations	Unrealistic expectations
Allowing freedom to try	Holding on to baby
Giving choices	Allowing no choices
Sending clear messages	Sending mixed messages
Focusing your attention	Neglecting your child
Offering nonjudgmental acceptance	Judging
Allowing for individuality	Demanding conformity
Having human limits and rules	Establishing demeaning rules
Being interested in child's interests	Showing no interest
Touching and loving	Name calling
Teaching problem-solving	Blaming child for all failures

7

THE
ADOLESCENT FAMILY

The quiet and calm of childhood end when your first child enters puberty. As adolescents enter into this period, many of the words which describe them will also describe the challenges faced by the family: stormy, changing, volatile, searching, rebelling, confusing, growing, thrilling, maturing, and developing.

An adolescent child grows so quickly and changes in so many ways that not only is the adolescent bewildered, but the parents and siblings are also confused. During this stage your adolescent is programmed to challenge and test your values, rules, power, control, and responsibility. The way in which you have resolved patterns of communication and boundaries in your family will set the scene for these interesting and demanding years.

Major Stresses

While your child is undergoing this complex, important stage of development, you may be at the same time undergoing your own midlife crisis. While your child is criticizing and questioning your values, life-style, goals, and dreams, you yourself may be questioning the same things. The arrogance of your adolescent may make this even more uncomfortable for you.

Yet you may benefit from the turmoil in your once peaceful household. This is an opportunity for both of you, the mother and the father, to reexamine your marriage, your career choices, your life dreams, and your priorities.

Other conflicts at this time may concern sexuality and elderly parents. As your adolescent is facing his or her burgeoning, confusing sexuality, you may be confused by your own waning sexuality. It is also common for parents, while facing the storm of adolescence, to be forced to cope with the illness or death of their own aging parents.

All of these stresses from within and without make this a challenging time for most families. If your marriage is based solely on your children, it is sure to be stressed as your children grow and prepare to leave home. For such families there isn't much left when the children leave.

The stresses of children and family life always take a toll on the intimacy of marriage. It takes time and energy to maintain a close and affectionate life. If the children's interests have superseded yours, you may be faced with a lifeless, sexless, affectionless marriage in which you have little in common with one another. If, as you progress through your own midlife experience, you and your mate are out of synch, your marriage may be stressed even further.

Usually the father is out of his thirties and now has a deep need for authenticity and genuineness. At the same time, the mother, having also passed through the thirties, may be thinking about stretching out professionally. In contrast to her husband's need for tenderness, she needs to become tougher, stronger, and more independent. Is it any wonder the marriage may be stressed?

Divorce statistics climb for families with adolescent children. And although adolescents may be an integral part of the reason for divorce, they may experience extreme pain and anger when their parents separate. They are pained by the end of a dream of a happy family, and they are angry that they become deprived of the affection and the support a whole family can give. They are frightened by the possibility of financial deprivation as they are confronted with rising costs of college. If there is a battle over custody and child support, the child resents becoming the battleground and will put emotional, if not physical, separation, between himself or herself and both parents to escape from the bitterness and hurt.

If there is a divorce, adolescent children are less hurt and have the best adjustment when both parents agree to put the child's benefits first and the child maintains a good relationship with the parent with whom he or she does not live.

Common Issues Confronting Adolescent Families

IMPORTANT

Each family will experience each adolescent differently, but there are recurring themes which seem to appear in most families. Probably the greatest issue confronting the adolescent family is the ongoing one of setting limits and letting go. Because adolescents have such a great deal of energy, the adolescent family may feel out of control and enervated. It is most important and very difficult to take the time for open communication, expressions of feelings, and the solving of problems. It is equally important that your family make special time to express appreciation of itself—appreciation of each member individually and of the family as a whole. Finances are another stress point. The raising of teens does require more money, and although most parents feel that teens should be out on their own earning at least a part of their spending money, it is difficult for unskilled teens to find jobs.

It is during the adolescent years that your family is probably at its greatest number, and sibling rivalry may be most acute. School may be stressful for teens and their parents, and issues of homework and curfew loom ominously in many households. Limitations and regulations have to be reassessed and brought up to date. Too rigid or too lenient rules are sure to cause problems in your family.

Few families are untouched by rebellious teenagers. Many have to deal with the big problems—drug use and abuse, teen sexuality and pregnancy, and rage and anger. Sexual promiscuity brings with it its own negative set of problems: venereal (socially transmitted) diseases, unwanted pregnancy, abusive relationships, and dealing with contraception for teens. Peer influence is profound for teens, and the choice of friends may become an issue; adolescents want the freedom to choose their own friends and will resist attempts of adults to supervise their choices.

Healthy Adolescent Family Patterns

Although most parents of an adolescent experience some stress, there are several positive patterns that develop in healthy families. First, the healthy family allows for the expanding boundaries of the adolescent without losing its grip on the situation. The tension of your grip on your child, in fact, is directly related to the degree of rebellion you can expect from that child. If you grip too tightly, your child will have to fight to find his or her precious identity. If you grip too lightly, your adolescent will be just as confused, with nothing on which to lean. A healthy family allows freedom, gives limits, lets the adolescent know that there is a family unit to depend on when he or she needs it. The teen may join in or be independent, but the family's integrity is not based on whether the teen is there or not.

A healthy family keeps open lines of clear communication and tries to send concise messages. This is a special time for helping adolescents set their own limits, for it won't be many years before they will be on their own making decisions and living with the consequences.

A healthy family works at building in fun and joy—because it can be awfully depressing for an adolescent on his or her own. Healthy families have parents who offer leadership and guidance to help their children develop into responsible adults. It takes a lot of patience, courage, and strength to set reasonable limits and watch adolescent children struggle with choices.

The greatest gift parents of adolescent children can give their family is a healthy marriage in which the parents act as role models. Together you communicate, solve problems, share power, love, and express compassion. These are the most valuable examples you can pass on to your children.

Family Patterns to Avoid

In a family where a leadership vacuum exists, the children will be enlisted into filling unhealthy roles. If the rigid authority exists only in one parent (such as the father), the submissive parent may unconsciously support rebellion and encourage the adolescent child to express the submissive parent's anger and hostility.

In a family in which the parents have used the child as a go-between in early stages, the adolescent may use his or her power as the go-between in destructive ways, both to himself or herself and to the parents. Blackmail strategies (in which either parent pays the child off to side with him or her), playing parents off against each other, being solely responsible for keeping the marriage together—these are unhealthy patterns for any child.

When a child has been involved in a triangle in adolescence the child may develop such habits as behaving outrageously, getting in trouble at school, getting into drugs or alcohol, or even joining strange nonconforming groups—the more outlandish, the better exposure. Labeled as "difficult," "delinquent," "ill-behaved," the child is only too willing to live up to the title. The problem child is working to hold the family together. But the price is high, and if the child becomes totally dependent on the unhealthy relationship, he or she can even be driven to suicide.

In early research on schizophrenic adolescents, researchers such as Gregory Bateson and Jay Haley began to explore family systems. As they looked into the complex patterns of roles, relationships, boundaries, and communication they began to view family dynamics and family therapy in a whole new way. They found that rigid families that consistently sent out mixed and confusing messages to their young could consistently produce mixed-up and confused adolescents. But which family member would be chosen to be the victim?

Through a hidden network of elaborate rules the family would choose a member to be the burden carrier. The family member who is the most sensitive and vulnerable plays into the game and allows himself or herself to be labeled the family rebel, victim, or troublemaker. This pathological pattern can be passed on from one generation to the next. Many families wait until adolescence to get therapy. The victim, of course, is the outward reason for counseling. They come in to get help because one child is revealing stress, when actually his or her behavior is a pressure valve to release tension that is building up within the family. As the adolescent is struggling for his or her identity, he or she is a vulnerable scapegoat for the troubled family. Tensions which may have been submerged in earlier stages of childhood are suddenly exaggerated in families that have problems dealing with adolescent children.

Jay Haley says it is not accidental that people most frequently go crazy—become schizophrenic—in the late teens and early twenties, at the time when the children are expected to leave home and the family is in turmoil. Adolescent schizophrenia and other severe disturbances can be seen as an extreme method of attempting to solve what happens to a family when parents and children cannot tolerate being separated; the threatened separation can be aborted if something goes wrong with the child.

By developing a problem that incapacitates him or her socially, the child remains within the family system. The parents can continue to share the child as a source of concern and disagreement, and they find it unnecessary to deal with each other without the child. The child can continue to participate in a triangular struggle with the parents, while offering his "mental illness" as an excuse for all difficulties. Some families in earlier childhood stages are so seriously flawed that they sacrifice their children to chronic mental illness.

In the family that cannot bear conflict, the victim becomes even more important in holding the family together. Nothing is wrong with the rest of the family, everyone is in harmony and love, but the victim is labeled crazy. This serves everyone in the enmeshed family—even the victim.

The Enmeshed Family. The enmeshed family has a terrible time allowing its boundaries to expand to fill the adolescent's deep need for independence. If this family has a child who has a powerful need for independence, there are sure to be troubled waters ahead. The family that has established a pattern of harmony at any cost—usually the cost of independence—cannot turn out a mature adult who is able to make adequate decisions. Families of this kind are not the happiest families. Because they cannot share feelings or concerns, family members cannot learn and solve problems with one another. The kind of cloying family that is all-loving and all-understanding, is the most difficult one for the teenager who needs someone with whom to share feelings and off whom to bounce problems. The child cannot grow up and out as the family enmeshes and squeezes out any opportunity for exploring and developing. The parents may exert excessive power to stay in control of their children and keep the children close to them.

The Disengaged Family. On the other hand, adolescence is a time for some families to "give up" on any attempt at being united. As the adolescent rebels, some parents cannot give the wise and mature leadership and discipline that adolescents so badly need if they are to develop into productive and healthy adults ready to leave home. This may manifest itself by excessively weak rules and regulations or by excessively rigid expectations. Both are destructive and dangerous to adolescent children struggling for ego identity. Both lead to emotional instability and role confusion.

In this family, each member is isolated and alone living out his or her needs, concerns, and experiences in a separate world. The adolescent, lacking both inner and outer discipline, is easily attracted to groups and experiences that are dangerous and threatening. Street gangs, fast driving, drinking, and drugs offer a way out in a world that is unstable and confusing. Gangs offer a sense of belonging, and drugs and drinking offer a dulling of pain and confusion. Unfortunately, this is the important period when children should be developing the mature ego which allows them to make decisions based on information and choice. Gangs and drugs are counterproductive to ego development and arrest the physically developed teen at a child's emotional level.

Understanding Your Adolescent Child

Task: Developing Ego Identity

Your adolescent is not a carbon copy of either of you, but a complex individual who has to find out who he or she is and what he or she is going to be. Although it will probably be a long and difficult period (some kids have longer and more difficult adolescences than others), all of the support and compassion you can give will be greatly appreciated—if not now, at least later. Everything seems to be happening at a dizzy rate— and the child may feel out of control as he or she grows and changes so quickly in so many ways. Maybe this is why adolescents spend so much time looking in mirrors and paying so much attention to appearance—because it's a stranger they're trying to get to know. Not only are their bodies changing until they hardly know themselves, but something is happening that makes them question things they never questioned before, and challenge ideas and people that they never challenged before.

Physical and Intellectual Growth. Height spurts up; weight is put on in different places; feet, nose, and facial features begin to take on adult proportions.

A boy is dealing with development of hair, muscles, and penis and testicles as they prepare to deliver the genetic material for the next generation. Sexuality takes on new meaning with highly erotic and sexual dreams (both awake and asleep). This sexuality isn't an accident, for in past times in mankind the adolescent male's aggressiveness was essential for the survival of the species. Now, however, if a boy unleashes uncontrolled sexuality, this ancient heritage may cause a lot of trouble.

A girl's physical development may be a source of joy or a source of sorrow to her as her body changes. Breasts and hips grow and body hair develops as internal reproductive organs prepare to deliver, protect, and nurture the next generation. Burgeoning sexuality affects her differently than adolescent males, and their aggressiveness is sometimes frightening to her.

Both males and females are all undergoing sporadic upsurges in hormones which affect emotions, sensations, and relations with others. Along with the tremendous hormonal and physical changes the adolescent experiences a tremendous spurt of new energy. These forces may cause a breakdown of obedience, but they also contribute to a new, more mature personality based on individual and unique needs.

Egocentric, same-sex love is replaced by sexual love for the opposite sex, and a deep sense of personal sexuality. In preparation for the sexuality of adulthood, the adolescent drives into opposite-sex relationships.

Adolescents crave new knowledge and experiences. Developing not only physically but intellectually, adolescents for the first time begin to master important conceptual and theoretical aspects of science and humanities, understand philosophy and other abstract fields, and use this information in thinking about what careers they want to pursue.

Adolescents are looking at and thinking about the world in new ways, considering other people's thinking, and wondering how other people feel about them.

They begin to ponder ideal families, religion, and societies and to compare these thoughts with the imperfections in their own parents, family, religion, and society as a reference point. Although you may be frustrated by continual questioning, confronting, and rebelling, it is important that you understand this is a normal part of your child's intellectual development, and when all is said and done, your child's values will probably be very close to yours.

One of the most exciting things that is happening is that the adolescent finds he or she is capable of constructing theories and philosophies. He or she may be interested in designing them to bring the conflicting aspects of society into a working, harmonious, and peaceful whole. The typical adolescent could be called an impatient idealist who believes that it is as easy to realize an ideal as it is to imagine it.

Social and Personal Growth. Adolescents are searching for identity. They want to find themselves to be people they can like, who are consistent (on whom they can count) and who

can bring together all of the things they learned about themselves as child, student, and friend. They need to integrate these
different images into a whole that makes sense and shows con-
tinuity with the past as they prepare for the future. They need
to know who they are, where they've been, and where they're
going.

If, thanks to you, your child has reached adolescence with
a sense of trust, independence, initiative, and productivity, then
his or her chances of arriving at a meaningful ego identity are
enhanced.

If your child enters adolescence with considerable mistrust,
shame, doubt, guilt and inferiority, the chances of passing
through adolescence without great storm and stress are less.
Unfortunate childhood experiences or difficult social circumstances will in all probability lead to a certain amount of role
confusion or a "negative identity" opposite to the one you may
want for him or her.

It's important, though, to realize that if adolescence has been
a difficult or negative time, it does not necessarily condemn a
child to perpetual failure. Nor does attaining a sense of identity
necessarily guarantee a life without further challenges or threats.
Life is constantly changing, and confronting problems at one
stage in life is not a guarantee against their reappearance later.
Ideally, we will be able to find new solutions to old problems
and conflicts.

During adolescence it is important to have intimate personal
relationships with friends of both the same and the opposite
sex. These relationships help a child to discover himself or
herself and how others view him or her. Through them the child
develops the skills needed for permanent relationships and
marriage.

Toward the end of this age, adolescents begin to think about
whom they want for a mate and what they would like to do in
life. They work on a life philosophy, which includes exploring
values and morals, share intimacy with friends, and begin to
pave the way for the more deeply satisfying personal relationships of early adulthood.

So uncertain about who they are, adolescents tend to need
and identify with an "in-group," sometimes even seeming to

be elitist, snobbish, intolerant, and cruel as they exclude others who are different. In a hurry to find some identity, adolescents may stereotype and align themselves with groups (be they social, religious, or political) which provide both an identity and a clear-cut image of good and bad in the world, and they may feel that they have to share all the opinions, judgments, values, morals, and dress of the group.

Parenting Tips

Your child now needs love, trust, and understanding more than ever before, plus all of your lessons in compassion, communication, problem-solving, faithfulness, negotiation, and love. He or she can only learn these skills as you, the greatest role models, show the way.

Two things trouble the child the most: the thought that he or she might not look good to others or meet other's expectations, and worries about his or her future place in the world. With rapidly expanding mental powers, a teen could easily feel overwhelmed by choices, options, and alternative.

In the struggle to develop a sense of identity, adolescents associate with those who appeal to them and desire to become like them. The best thing that can happen to an adolescent is to find a mentor (other than parents or friends) who cares about him or her and gives positive guidance. An adolescent also develops a sense of self through accomplishments.

Even though identity formation will be a lifelong process, adolescence may be a time of crises. Sometimes the inability to make lasting commitments is painful. And sometimes the child will be overwhelmed when there is too much to decide, too soon.

Until adolescents know who they are and what they will do in life, they will feel isolated with a feeling that time is passing them by and occasionally feel unable to find meaning in any kind of activity. Although this is painful, healthy adolescents know intuitively that the search for identity will lead to understanding. Please hang in there with your teen.

Actions That Encourage Ego Identity— and Actions That Promote Role Confusion

EGO IDENTITY	ROLE CONFUSION
Letting go	Holding on too tight
Human rules	Too lenient rules
Flexible rules	Too rigid rules
Trusting child	Distrusting
Setting limits	No limits
Permitting experimentation	Stifling
Accepting individuality	Forcing family conformity
Giving clear messages	Double binds (mixed messages)
Giving responsiblity	Expecting no responsiblity
Allowing child to face consequences	Allowing no mistakes
Realistic expectations	Unrealistic expectations
Negotiating with child	Not negotiating
Helping problem-solving	Solving all child's problems
Physical affection	Lack of affection
Verbalizing appreciation	Showing no appreciation
Praising successes	Putting down child
Allowing choice in friends	Putting friends down
Allowing for identity search	Ridicule
Giving choices	Allowing no choices
Allowing for differences	Comparing to other kids
Giving information on sexuality	Keeping sexuality secret or dirty
Providing supportive environment	Unsupportive environment
Listening actively	Ignoring child
Providing positive reinforcement	Hitting and yelling

8

THE LAUNCHING FAMILY

Children who have successfully maneuvered from infancy throuh adolescence are now able to move on to the challenges of adulthood. As adolescents, they were concerned about who they were, how they appeared in the eyes of others, and what they would become. In their interactions they were trying to find out who they were, endlessly talking about their true feelings, their views of others, their plans, hopes, and expectations. They were too preoccupied with who they were to experience true intimacy.

Real intimacy is possible only after children have developed a sense of identity. It is only after they are sure of their identity that they are able to experience a mature love with another. If they marry before they have established a strong sense of identity, their marriage has less chance to succeed. They cannot expect to live intimately with another person until they have become themselves. True intimacy is possible only when people are willing to share and mutually resolve all important aspects of their lives. The danger of this period is that they may not be ready for the demands of intimacy and may retreat into personal isolation. When they achieve self-awareness they will be able to find a partner with whom they can share opinions and judgments, and with whom they can establish a promising, productive, and procreative life.

Letting Go

In healthy families the marriage is strong enough to weather the departure of the first child. In fact, many people feel that their marriage becomes warmer and better after the children start to leave. If your marriage is troubled and only has meaning with the existence of children, when the children leave you may be disconcerted to find that you are living with a stranger.

During this period, as you are watching your children leave, you may reexamine your relationship with your own parents. If you are in your own midlife crises, or if you are confronted with ill or dying parents, the vacancy left by a child may overwhelm you. If the mother has built her life around her children, she may experience the "empty-nest syndrome" and be confused without her role as mother. If the mother has taken on other roles in preparation for this stage of her life, she will tend to view her children's leaving more positively, and allow them the space they need.

Letting go of them as children both in your own and in their eyes can be difficult. You have been practicing for this during the child's life, however. Letting go of your toddler was only a beginning, and you finish the task as you launch your young adults. How your children have developed trust, independence, initiative, industry, and identity will determine how they leave the family.

Sometimes families that have experienced the other developmental stages with relative equanimity are shocked by the reality of the young adult's leaving home. It is during this stage that the family experiences the most radical transformation. How each family reacts to this departure will depend on its own individual style. Enmeshed families tend to let go grudgingly and slowly. Disengaged families tend to push their child out of the nest early and abruptly. Disturbed families hold on with every strategy possible (including physical and mental illness on the part of the parents or the child).

IMPORTANT

Issues Confronting the Launching Family

The major issues confronting the family that is asked to let go of its children and launch them into adulthood are age-old: power, independence, self-esteem, and sexuality.

Siblings have to reorganize their roles when one in the family unit leaves. Emotions are running high and feelings need to be expressed.

For children to leave with a feeling of high self-esteem, they must be sure of their identity and successes, and know that they can turn to their parents for support and guidance when necessary.

Healthy Launching Families

The healthy family lets its children leave with a feeling of love, affection, and goodwill. Parents are able to turn over power to their children and accept them as equal adults. They can renegotiate the boundaries and let go of a child, while at the same time willingly taking in that child's marriage partner. While letting go, parents are able to let their children know they can come back to the family for support and guidance at any time. The healthy family launches children who have skills in clear communications and who know how to solve problems on their own. Freedom and independence are accepted as the children are granted adult status in the family.

Family Patterns to Be Avoided

As the child leaves, any unhealthy family pattern that has been developing in the family throughout the life cycle comes to a head. In fact, unhealthy family patterns tend to become more intense with each successive generation.

The launching child who feels responsible for holding the marriage together cannot help but be affected in his or her quest to become a mature adult. Such children may have become so helpless, fearful, and dependent on their parents that they cannot leave home.

In enmeshed families in which members have become harmonious to the extent that conflict is avoided at any cost (including avoiding anger), rebellion or hostility is stifled. The children may then be incapable of separating themselves from the family. If the child leaves and the parents try to control the young adult with power or money, the child's search for himself or herself is very prolonged. On the other hand, it is just as important for children to realize that they may come home again for advice and support if they find themselves in less than desirable circumstances. In the safety of home they can work things out with their parents, and leave again on a more positive note. For this to happen, the parents have to face the fact that their children are becoming adults. The parents must give up their old strategies of keeping their children attached to them.

Becoming In-laws

As your children bring their choices for mates home, it is up to you and the family to include the new mates.

There are many ways the family of origin can help the children as young adults and newlyweds. The new marriage is fragile and precious, and parents can give support and encouragement to the new couple. Parents should allow them space to live their own lives while still providing the spoken and unspoken support and assistance they need. Clear communication and expressions of love and appreciation help enhance a new marriage.

An unhealthy family unit can blur the new marriage, and repeat cloying and absorbing ways. This may diminish the new partners' abilities to grow and develop as individuals and as spouses. Parents may use money and power to buy off the newlyweds only to find that their help is not appreciated.

Disengaged families are unable to accept the new member of the family. The coldness and distance of the parents leaves the new daughter- or son-in-law in the cold. If the son or daughter cannot support his or her partner emotionally, their marriage is sure to be in trouble.

Becoming Grandparents

Your children's pregnancies and the births of your grandchildren will affect you deeply. You now assume a new role in life as grandparents. Many times, if there has been alienation during the adolescent or early adulthood stage, the oncoming birth will be an opportunity for children and their parents to come together under new and more understanding terms. If you're the mother, you will relive your own pregnancies and births and all they meant to you. And if you are the father, you will take on new appreciation for the adult status of your children. As parents, you may feel new pride of being part of the magnificent turnover of generations.

Grandchildren bring in a new and rewarding stage of life for many grandparents in which integrity and wisdom take on new meaning. Your emotional, physical, intellectual, and spiritual assistance may enhance the new family unit. Daughters may find their mothers more supportive and helpful. Sons and fathers also discover themselves in a closer relationship. Mothers- and fathers-in-law who offer nonjudgmental support and sincere appreciation to their daughters- and sons-in-law may bring joy to both the grandchildren and the new family. Grandmothers who are active and busy with their own lives get pleasure from their grandchildren, and many grandfathers enjoy a chance to be the caretakers that they were not able to be with their own children.

On the other hand, bitter and disappointed parents may not be able to rise to a higher level in their own lives, and may react by sabotaging the new family unit. When the new generation is born, old, destructive family patterns may find new and fertile soil. Scapegoating, triangulation, and mixed messages will go on generation after generation unless consciously examined and definitely stopped.

Research shows that mothers-in-law who are not able to accept new daughters-in-law and who express their disapproval and disappointment are sure to be perceived as interfering and disruptive to the marriage and to the grandchildren. Fathers-in-law who are not able to accept their daughter's husband and who are negative in their judgment and perception of the husband can also be disruptive to the marriage.

When grandparents are able to relax and enjoy the experience of grandparenting, and put behind them their own disappointments and midlife crises, they are able to enter into a new level of appreciation. Sometimes the grandmother-granddaughter relationship and the grandfather-grandson relationship is closer than the original mother-daughter, father-son relationships. Many grandparents express pleasure at having grandchildren without the responsibility of raising them. Without the pressures and financial obligations of parenthood, there is no need to be perfect or set impossible standards. Grandparents can be important in developing high self-esteem in their grandchildren because they are nonthreatening and nonjudgmental in their love.

PART II

FAMILY SKILLS

9

COPING WITH UNIVERSAL PROBLEMS

There are universal family problems that are persistent and predictable—problems of coping with differences in attitudes and expectations concerning money, sex, religion, discipline, work, and leisure time.

All families encounter problems. In fact, the problems your family faces carry within them important lessons. Children learn either that problems are growth-producing or that they can be destructive. The difference between healthy and unhealthy families is not the problems, but how the families perceive themselves (high or low self-esteem); how they handle power (flexibly or rigidly); how they communicate (in healthy or destructive ways); and what kinds of expectations parents have for themselves and their children (realistic or unrealistic).

My experience with mothers and fathers has shown that almost all parents want to do a good job and are sincerely doing the best they can with the tools they have inherited from their own families. I always recommend that parents put away guilt and realize that they really have done the best they can with what they have. What I do propose is that any positive family living can be enhanced by improving the quality of their parenting skills.

This means being sensitive to how your children perceive themselves and developing insights and skills that will enable you to help your family bolster its self-esteem, devise workable rules and regulations for itself, improve its communication skills, and make its expectations more realistic.

And that is what the rest of this book is all about.

Family of Origin

With care, concern, and good parenting, a child's chances of becoming a healthy and happy human being increase. Each family has its own style of facing the universal stresses that come with each stage of life. If, by chance, your parents gave you healthy, unconflicting messages on these issues and you find a mate who shares these same messages, you are sure to bypass many of the pitfalls of family strife. No family, however, can give children only healthy messages during their childhood.

During courtship, of course, you are not attracted to a person because of his or her past family messages on these subjects, and even if there is an obvious difference you both take little notice of it. During the honeymoon, slight differences may begin to surface, but love still maintains a state of harmony. After the honeymoon, the full personality of the person you married emerges and the issues of family life create either a battlefield or a relationship in which you can both grow and learn from each other.

Common Relationships

Let's take a look at the messages different families of origin can pass on and how they can sow seeds of mutuality or seeds of strife.

Look at your own family of origin. Think a little bit about your mother. Under what circumstances was she born? What place did she hold in her own family? How did these experiences shape her views on life? Now think about your father. Under what circumstances was he born? What place did he hold in his own family? How did these experiences shape his views on life? The messages they received from their parents about money, sex, show of affection, religion, work, discipline, work, and leisure and any conflicts they had between them are the same messages you brought into your marriage. These messages in themselves are neither right nor wrong, nor do they necessarily predict stress; they only carry the potential for stress. The potential is fulfilled only when you marry a person who received different, conflicting messages from his or her own parents.

Money. What messages did your mother give you about money? What messages did your father give you about money? What conflicting messages did you get about money? How did it affect your view of money? What messages did your spouse get about money? How are they different? How are they conflicting? How do the conflicts affect your marriage?

Sue received messages that money is to enjoy and spend. Her parents both agreed and never fought; they just enjoyed life. If Sue had married someone who had received similar messages, money would not have been an issue in their lives. But she chose Bill, who received messages from his father to save and spend wisely. His mother believed in spending, and his parents fought continually. Bill was appalled by Sue's spending habits, and money became a constant battle much as it had been in Bill's childhood.

Joan came into marriage with the message to save and put away for a rainy day. John came with the same message. Money was not an issue in their marriage.

Sex and Sexuality. What messages did your mother give you about sex, sexuality, and displaying affection? What messages did you get from your father? Were there any conflicts between your parents concerning sex? How did this affect you? What messages do you have about sex? What messages did your spouse get from his or her parents? How has this affected your relationship?

Hanny came from a family which was naturally affectionate, and sexuality and sex were an accepted and normal part of life. Though it wasn't spoken openly, Hanny remembers her father patting her mother on the fanny and kissing her in front of the

kids. William came from a family where he remembers his
father saying "Don't get caught," and his mother thinking anything sexual was nasty. Throughout their marriage Hanny has
complained about William's inability to express the affection
she needs. And as William has begun to withdraw from her
constant demands, sex has become a central issue in their
household.

Religion, Spirituality, and Morals. What messages did your
mother give you about religion? What messages did you get
about spirituality and morals (for example, about lying, stealing,
cheating)? What messages did you get from your father? Were
there any conflicting messages? What messages do you have
about religion, spirituality, morals? What messages did your
spouse get? How do they affect your relationship?

Anita was raised by a family with a strong, traditional Cath-
olic background. She and John had met at school during their
junior year. Although John came from a Baptist background, he
converted to Catholicism for Anita. They both agreed to raise
their children in the church, and were devoted members of the
parish. Church was a strength in their marriage.

Karen was raised in the Jewish faith and attended Jewish
schools until graduation. At the university she met and fell in
love with Jim, who came from a family of Episcopalians. Church
had not been important in his life; he thought of himself more
as an agnostic or aetheist, and didn't care to get involved in
any church. After the children came, Kathy felt alone in raising
her children Jewish, while Bill felt left out. Religion became a
power issue separating the family.

Discipline and Raising Children. What were the messages
your mother gave you about discipline? What were the messages
your father gave you about discipline? Was there any conflict
in these messages? What were the messages your spouse got
from his or her parents? Is there any conflict? How has it affected
your relationship?

Franny and Tod were deeply in love. They attended
prepared-childbirth classes together, and Tod himself delivered

their second child. They seemed to be perfectly matched. There were no issues of money, sex, or religion between them. However, as the first child neared the age of the terrible twos, a rift suddenly appeared. Tod had been raised in a traditional German family where discipline was a way of life. On the other hand, Franny came from an easygoing family that believed in letting children discipline themselves. Tod thought that Franny was just too permissive with their oldest son when she let him draw all over the walls, and he was upset that she hadn't even begun to toilet-train him. Franny thought Tod a brute for wanting to use force on their baby. Their fights over discipline soon became a major issue in their relationship.

Work and Leisure Time. What were your mother's messages about work and leisure time? What were your father's messages about work and leisure time? Were there any conflicts between them concerning work roles and how to use leisure time? How did this affect your view of work or of leisure time? What were the messages your spouse got from his or her family? Are there any conflicts between your views of work and leisure time? How has this affected your relationship?

Katy came from a family whose mother never worked outside the home. Her father was independently wealthy, and family leisure time was valued. She met and married Daniel, whose mother and father, although wealthy, had started from a poor background. Work was the family altar. When Daniel went into business with his father, Katy was delighted. After all, she did enjoy the finer things of life. But she didn't bargain on Daniel's falling into the family work ethic of working ten hours a day, six days a week, and being on call the seventh. She resented his being gone, and he resented her lack of appreciation for his efforts. Work became a central issue between Katy and Daniel, who were divorced in the third year of their marriage.

Vacation time is a nightmare in the home of the Smiths. Helen came from a family where vacation meant "vacation" (Mexico, California, Hawaii). Steve came from a family where vacation meant a week on a camping trip and then home to work on the lawn. As the kids came along, all of them had their own ideas, some siding with Mom, others with Dad. Vacation time meant a time of stress and fighting rather than rest and relaxation for this family.

Do any of the above situations sound familiar? They are the most universal areas where people work out issues of who is in power. Who makes the rules? Who has the independence? Who feels unappreciated and has fears and unmet needs?

Luckily, you are not doomed to live a life of fighting over issues that are destructive to your family's health. Recognizing problems is the first step toward learning to cope with them.

10

A PLACE IN YOUR FAMILY

What Position Means to Your Parenting

The order in which your child is born into your family will have a great effect on his or her experience as a member of the family. The more you can understand how your children perceive themselves, their siblings, and their position in the family, the more effective your parenting can be. You will be able to avoid some problems, and make meaningful adjustments.

The order of birth influences your parenting style, your expectations, your manner of discipline, and even your relationship to each child. Your own birth order and your perception of yourself will also come into play. In addition, each child in your family views you as parents from wherever he or she is in the birth order. Equally, each child views and reacts to siblings from his or her own viewpoint.

Circumstances may change, depending on whether the child is a boy or girl, the sexes of the other children in the family, and the differences in ages between the children. Any instances of death, miscarriage, stillbirth, illness, or retardation of other children born either before or after the child are also important factors.

The consistency of how oldest children feel about themselves, how middle children view themselves, and finally how babies of the family see themselves is just too important for parents to overlook. The viewpoint of only children is just as consistent in affecting how they develop as adults.

In a recent research project, over two thousand men, women, and children reported their perceptions about themselves and their siblings. When asked how they felt about their birth order, what they liked about it and what they would like to change, and what messages they would like to pass on to other parents, their responses were amazing in similarity and consistency. It's important that parents listen to their answers and take them into consideration as they parent their children.

Sibling Positions in the Family

Oldest
Second of two
Middle (second, third, etc.)
Only Child

Variables Affecting Family Position

Spacing
  (More than five years)
Physical/mental illness
Death
  (Miscarriage/stillbirth)
Blended families
Adoption

Gender of child
  (Wanted/unwanted)
First boy/second girl
First girl/second boy
Only boy of girl family
Only girl of boy family
Twins

Scripting: Labels the Family May Place on Its Members

Dependable
Responsible
Troublemaker
Peacemaker
The Brain
The Joker
The Manipulator
The Spoiled Baby

Winner
Loser
Martyr
Scatterbrain
Little Mother/Father
Princess/Prince
The Rebel
The "Problem" Child

Oldest Child

Oldest children are unique because at one time they knew the undiluted love of their parents. The birth of the second child leaves an indelible mark on the first child. First children almost always find the power, control, and authority they hold over the rest of the family the most important aspect of their position.

What It's Like to Be Firstborn. Firstborns like being the first to have new clothes, new toys, and other possessions. The thing they like least is all of the responsibility they must sometimes assume while at the same time being the "pioneer" for the rest of the family. They feel that their parents' expectations were greater and discipline more unrealistic. Many times siblings see the firstborn as helpful and loving, and yet also threatening, intimidating, and judgmental.

First children usually describe themselves as:

The Dependable One
The Responsible One
Old Faithful
The Perfectionist
The Student
The Little Mother/Father
The Big Sister/Brother
The Protector of the Family
The Prince/Princess of the Family
The Family's Only Hope

Because of many complex factors, first children often take positions of leadership as adults. A large majority of doctors and politicians, for example, are first children.

Messages to Parents. A first child often wants to tell his or her parents:

"Stop making me so responsible for the rest of the family."

"Don't be so rigid and have such high expectations for me. I either can't or won't live up to them, or I will kill myself trying to be perfect."

"Allow me more mistakes, and the consequences of my actions."

"Don't think you can live your own high expectations through my successes; and don't take my failures so personally."

Messages to Siblings. The firstborn often wants to tell younger siblings:

"Grow up and don't be so immature."

"Don't make me do all the work."

"Why don't you take on some of the responsibilities around here?"

Special Problems for the Firstborn. If the firstborn is followed by a second child who is smarter, larger, brighter, or more social, the first may perceive himself or herself as less powerful and more vulnerable.

Second Child

Your second child comes along with an unalterable liability: The first child will always see him or her as the usurper, as the enemy who took away Mom and Dad's unmitigated love and attention. While the second child is innocent and small, the large and plotting first child may never give up trying to show Mom and Dad how really inadequate the second child is. Your first child may even try to hit, abuse, or even get rid of the second child. The abuse may be physical at first and emotional later. The second child, unaware of how to fight, may turn to tactics such as crying, whining, lying, backbiting, or subtle sabotaging to protect himself or herself against such a large and overwhelming antagonist. Though normal, this pattern can go

on forever; sibling rivalry among eighty-year-olds is not un-
known.

What It's Like to Be a Second Child. Second children like
it that their older sibling has already blazed the trail. They enjoy
having an older sister or brother to take care of them and help
them when they need it. They do not, however, like having
hand-me-downs. They do not like it when the oldest is forever
superior—and lets everyone know it.

Their perception of their role in the family is often as:

The Rebel
The Social One
The Clown
The Entertainer
The Artistic One
The Behavior Problem
The Troublemaker
The Loser
The Peacemaker
The Negotiator

A majority of lawyers (trying to get some kind of justice in an
unfair world) and entertainers are second children, perhaps in
reaction to the complicated messages the second child receives
growing up.

Messages to Parents. Second children want their parents to
know that they need special care:

"Give me more attention."
"Spend more time with me."
"Have higher expectations of me."
"Don't compare me to my older brother or sister."
"Let me be myself with all my own individual and unique
qualities."
"Take me out by myself without all my siblings around me."
"Talk to me more to find out what I'm like."
"Don't ask my older brother or sister for advice about me."

"Don't let my older brother or sister boss me around so much."
"Don't put my older sibling in charge of me."

Messages to Siblings. To older siblings, messages are apt to be:

"Don't be so bossy."
"Don't be so critical and judgmental."
"Thanks for helping me when I needed it."
"Thanks for being there."

To younger siblings, one message may be:
"Thank you for allowing me to be an older sibling to you."

Middle Child

Your middle child never knew what it was like to be the only adored one, nor what it is like to be the second and left out. Most middle children express their relief at being the middle, not overwhelmed by their parents' high or low expectations.

What It's Like to Be a Middle Child. Most middle children feel that their parents have mellowed by the time they came along. They are allowed to be a unique and different person. They feel that nothing, including their successes, shakes their parents up very much. The one thing they don't like is the hand-me-down syndrome, and they feel that they really never get anything new—only used.

Middle children many times see themselves as:

The Easy One
The Dependable One
The Independent One
The Negotiator
The Easygoing One
The Nonperfectionist

The Peacemaker
The Independent One

Middle children usually are comfortable in independent occupations. They are in business and professional areas, and many middle children are writers.

Messages to Parents. Middle children's messages to their parents usually are:

"Try to get a little more excited about my accomplishments."
"I know my sisters and brothers have done everything before me—but this is the first in my life."
"If there is one thing I'm tired of, it's hand-me-downs—please buy me something new."
"Try to leave the other kids at home and take me out by myself once in a while."

Messages to Siblings. These are usually different for older siblings and younger ones:

"To my older brothers and sisters, thanks for all the support and help you gave me."
"To my baby siblings, I'm usually glad to help you, but stay out of my room, keep out of my things, and please respect my privacy."

Baby of the Family

The baby of the family is usually a special thing to behold. Realizing this is the last one, both the parents and the siblings ask for little and give much to this prize possession. Babies often have learned ways of getting what they want without coming into direct conflict with authority because they have accepted their older siblings' leadership and authority.

What It's Like to Be a Baby. By the time the baby of the family comes along, parents are usually in a better financial position. Babies love all the attention and material possessions that are heaped on them. Most babies love the special place they hold in the family and feel confident of their skills to charm and manipulate anyone in the family. They are accustomed to getting their way, and are charming when not crossed. Babies agree, however, that they do not like being called "the baby." They dislike not being taken seriously by anyone. They want their opinions and their knowledge to be respected.

Babies of the family often see themselves in a very precious light, playing roles that could be described as:

The Little One
The Lucky One
The Charmed One
The Manipulator
The Cute One
Peter Pan
The Spoiled One
The Sweet One
The One with the Terrible Temper

Because babies of families are used to accepting leadership in others, they often find occupations in more passive and submissive fields. Many times babies of the family do not want to grow up, and remain "cute kids" throughout their lives.

Messages to Parents. Babies of the family have many consistent messages they would like their parents to know:

"Please take me seriously."
"Treat me like a grown-up."
"Give me more responsibility."
"Listen to my ideas and opinions."
"Let me grow up."
"Don't always apologize for me; let me take the consequences of my actions."

Messages to Siblings. These are similar to messages to parents:

"Please take me more seriously."
"Please give more respect."

Only Child

The position of an only child is a remarkable one. The reason the child is the only one—whether the size of the family is planned, whether the parents have lost other children to miscarriage, stillbirth, or death, or whether the parents could not have other children—is a factor in how the only child views himself or herself, and how the parents perceive the child.

What It's Like to Be an Only Child. Only children agree that they like the peace and quiet of their position. They like not having to share and not having to fight for their rights. They regret not having the companionship of siblings, although many like being the only child and wouldn't trade it for anything. They feel tremendous pressure from their parents as the "only hope" in the family. As parents age, only children have no one else with whom to share their burden of caring for the parents.

Only children many times label themselves as:

The Loner
The Responsible One
The Lucky One
The Unlucky One
The Perfect One
The Fragile One
The Important One
The Prince/Princess
The Strange One
The Different One

Messages to Parents. Only children want to tell their parents:

"Please ease the pressure."

"Accept the fact that my successes—and failures—are not yours nor a reflection on you."

"Don't personalize my life into yours."

"Give me space to be myself."

"Allow me to have friends and relatives to make up for my loneliness, and to give me social skills."

11

SELF-ESTEEM
AND APPRECIATION

In order to cope with universal family problems, a family needs rules and regulations and communication skills. But for the rules to be effective and for the skills to work, you first must find ways to express self-esteem and appreciation in a family.

What Is Self-Esteem?

The basis of your family style, structure, and systems is determined by how the members of the family feel about themselves, about the parent unit, and about the family itself. Self-esteem is an integral part of a healthy person, a healthy marriage, and a healthy family.

What is this thing called self-esteem and how do you get it? Self-esteem is self-respect, a feeling of being important, of value, of worth. It is a person's regard for himself or herself. Self-esteem affects how partners feel about each other and their marriage and how members view their family unit.

As a basis for feeling loved and appreciated, self-esteem affects a person's and family's creativity, stability, and integrity. A person's feeling of self-worth forms the core of his or her own personality. It is the center of a healthy marriage, and it is a basis for how a family functions. High self-esteem is a crucial element in a healthy family. Low self-esteem is sure to be found in a troubled family.

How Do You Get It?

Where does self-esteem come from, and how do you give it to your children? Although all people are born with the potential for acquiring self-worth, not everyone finds it.

Self-esteem develops from earliest childhood experiences and memories of discovery of self. It comes from the messages of love, caring, appreciation, and respect parents pass on to their children. It is a feeling of self-worth that you gain as you move on in life. Successes and failures become a part of how you view yourself and influence your choice of a marriage partner and your expectations for your marriage and family. You pass on those messages of self-worth and esteem to your children.

High Self-Esteem. If the messages you received in your own childhood were full of hope and faith and respect, you probably chose a mate who had similar messages, and together you pass on to your children high self-worth. The atmosphere you create for your family is probably one in which appreciation and love are loud and clear. Individual differences are appreciated and mistakes are tolerated. Your communications patterns are open, concise, and dependable. The rules in your family are probably humane in that you trust the members to do the things that are right for them and the family.

Low Self-Esteem. If the first messages you received from your parents were negative and you felt unloved and unwanted, or, if your first needs were not attended to with warmth and concern, you may have developed feelings of low self-esteem. These feelings would be reinforced by an attitude of inadequacy to master and achieve skills. It could affect your view of yourself and whom you choose as a mate to mirror your feelings of inadequacy.

Since you tend to parent as you were parented, you may pass on to your children your feelings of inadequacy and low self-esteem. Your family may reflect these feelings with an environment of inflexibility, rigidity, crooked communication patterns, and expressions of blaming and criticism rather than appreciation and warmth.

Individual Self-Esteem

You can't give self-esteem to your children or marriage partner until you have high self-esteem for yourself. Even if you were fortunate enough to receive high self-esteem in your childhood, once you become involved in the giving of marriage and the overwhelming tasks of parenting, you may find your self-esteem shaky.

If your parents were not able to provide the lessons of self-esteem, however, you are not doomed. There are things you can do now which will help revitalize that important part of your personality. It is important to your marriage and your family that you initially spend special time doing those things which will enrich your feelings of value and worth as a person.

How Do You Show Self-Appreciation?

Low self-esteem comes partially from a sense of being in a life of drudgery, boredom, and rigid practicality. You may see yourself as a fool, a martyr, a slave. High self-esteem comes from the creative, playful, and celebrating part of you.

What can you do to bring on feelings of self-respect, dignity, and high self-esteem? To find out what makes you feel good, start with those experiences that give you a natural high about yourself. You will probably find yourself thinking about experiences that involve thrill, creativity, courage, vitality, enthusiasm, risk-taking, energy, and effort.

Here are some thoughts husbands and wives have shared with me on things they do to reinforce positive feelings about themselves—little things and big things, things that they take time to do to make themselves more whole and more able to give and receive love.

What I Do to Help My Self-Esteem: As a Woman, Wife, and Mother

"I find that if I can just get out and be alone for a few hours, I am rejuvenated. I can look at myself, my marriage, and my kids with more objectivity and not so much self-pity."

"I like going back to school and taking classes that I love, like anthropology. They're not going to get me anywhere, but they make me feel good."

"I sew and create, away from husband and kids. Just being alone and creating really turn me on."

"I go out and get my hair done and a facial. I know it sounds corny, but it's doing something just for me."

"I walk in the woods, all by myself. The sound of crisp leaves under my feet, the smell of the pine tar, a crisp blue sky give me space to be myself."

"I disappear into the bathroom, lock the door, draw a bath, put in bubble-bath oil, pour myself a glass of wine, and just luxuriate with my favorite book."

"Shopping, shopping, shopping. There is something therapeutic about shopping and buying something new. It may be expensive, but my husband says it's cheaper than a psychiatrist."

"I call up a friend and we go out to lunch and share our problems and our joys."

"I was overwhelmed with everything and felt so bad that I went to a counselor, who helped me a lot. And that's what I do for me—I go to my counselor and don't feel guilty about the money I am spending on me for me."

"Every Wednesday night I go out and teach a class to expectant parents. I leave my husband and kids behind and go out and talk like an adult with adults."

"I just went back to work after staying home three years. We could sure use the money. But I didn't do it for that. I did it for me and my sanity. I feel I'm a better wife and mother for it."

"Every Tuesday night, I leave my husband and kids and go

to my dance class. It's not for anybody but me—but I come home a new person seeing my life in a new way."

"I treat myself and go to a conference, workshop, or meeting which can help me learn and grow."

"I teach at the senior citizens' center every week. It gets me away from the kids and lets me be an adult for one night a week. It makes me feel good to give something to older people."

"I go to a women's support group, where I can say what I feel and get help in sorting out my problems. It gives me a cleaner feeling, and I can go back to life with a feeling that I'm not alone."

What I Do to Help My Self-Esteem: As a Man, Husband, and Father

"Every chance I get I go out hiking in the mountains. It lets me get out and commune with nature. Things just sort of fall in place for me afterward."

"I find that I can relax and escape sitting in front of the TV watching some mindless football game. It lets me get away."

"I can relax best out on the golf course. All the cares of the day, week, and month leave me, and I just concentrate on playing the best game I can."

"I have an old motorcycle that I get on and just ride off into the sunset. Nothing else gives me such a feeling of well-being."

"When things get rough, I go out and work on any car I can get my hands on. It seems as my mind becomes so absorbed with figuring out whatever is wrong and fixing it, I can leave everything else behind."

"I have a shop in my basement. It has all my dad's old woodworking tools in it, and when I go down and begin to putter and feel something come out of a piece of wood in my hands, it gives me something special."

"Well, I like to go out and buy clothes—just like my wife. It gives me a real feeling of pleasure to buy something. You might call it selfish—but it does the job for me."

"I've got a standing date with a bunch of fellows to play

poker every Monday night. Come hell or high water we're all there. It's not just the poker, it's the company and support and trust we've got going for ourselves."

"I'm one of those crazy mountain climbers. You ask me why climb that mountain—and I'll tell you because it's there and it really gives me a high. I leave everything behind down on the ground, and just concentrate on the climb. It's real exhilaration."

"All those stories about jogging and endorphins are true. I get out there alone and really stretch. It feels great and I feel great."

"I'm another sports enthusiast. Waterskiing in the summer, downhill and cross-country skiing in the winter. They are all my escapes—the time when I feel good about myself."

"I lock myself in my study, get a glass of beer, my pipe, and a good book, and lose myself for a few hours. The book is a pretext, because I don't want to see anyone or talk to anyone—just be alone. And then I can come back."

"I direct our church choir on the weekends—it gives me a great sense of giving and getting. It's a special time for me."

"I've been coaching Little League—and it's a great way to escape. I love watching the kids learn and grow. We never win a game—but that's not what it's about anyway."

What Do You Do to Enhance Self-Esteem in Your Marriage?

Almost all of us began with dreams of having a marriage in which each partner supported and enriched a caring relationship. To realize such a dream both partners must work at fostering self-esteem and expressing appreciation. Look carefully at your own marriage; and while you are at it, look at your parents' marriage as well. They were your most powerful role models, and you probably will recreate their problems unless you consciously decide to do differently.

How do you express affection, appreciation and caring—the things self-esteem is made of—to your partner? How does your partner express it to you? Have you built in ways to express appreciation, ways to ask for appreciation, and ways to exchange expressions of love and affection?

Although such expression may come easily during the courtship days, when most people are on their best behavior and giving their best shots at impressing, it does not continue to come easily during the stresses of marriage and parenting. In fact, it gets harder and harder as responsibilities and stresses get stronger and stronger. Loving each other isn't enough. Couples have to work, and work hard, at making their marriage relationship warm, caring, and mutually giving. That means you have to be as creative at enriching your marriage as you do at keeping your own self-esteem. If you are not careful, your marriage can become as dull as your own life.

To keep the marriage alive and exciting and full of high self-esteem, we all have to bring forth our creative, playing, and celebrating self to find ways of showing appreciation to each other both verbally and nonverbally. What are the ways you and your spouse express appreciation to each other? In what little (and big) ways do you let each other know that you care for and love each other? How do you show each other that you are the most important person in each other's life?

Here are a few ways of enriching each other's lives that wives and husbands have shared with me.

Wives: Ways We Enrich Our Marriages

"My husband and I have a standing date every Friday night. We found that if we didn't, we never got out of the house alone. It's kept the romance in our marriage."

"I pack love notes in my husband's lunch so that while he unwraps his sandwich—or whatever—he knows how much I love and appreciate him."

"My husband loves golf, and to show my appreciation, I let him go every weekend to play golf without making him feel guilty (even though I hate it!)."

"I sent my husband a bouquet of roses at his office and signed it 'Your mistress.' He loved it."

"I rub my husband's back and give him a massage when I feel especially loving. It's great for both of us."

"My greatest gift is to leave my husband alone when he needs it. I walk out of the room, take the kids, and give him the needed time alone."

"When my husband wants to make love and I don't, I get pleasure by giving him pleasure because I know it's important to him."

"I make my husband his favorite meal and serve it by candlelight."

"I have my husband's family over even though I don't get along with them. I know he appreciates it."

"I go along with my husband to football games when he has no one else to go with because it's a way I can give him company at the game."

"My gift to my husband was getting him to go along for marriage counseling, where we learned to work out our problems together."

"I try to keep my mouth shut about things he doesn't want to talk about, like his family, because I know how it makes him feel bad."

"I know that my husband likes it when I tell him 'thank you' for all the things he has done for me and the kids. I know he's given up a lot, and I really appreciate it."

"I tell my husband the things I love about him: I love the way he jokes and makes me laugh. I love the way he takes me camping and carries the heaviest load."

"I kidnapped my husband. I had packed our bags, made reservations at a motel, got a baby-sitter; and Friday night when he walked out of his office, I was there in the car. We drove off and I didn't tell him where we were going. He immediately got into the game—and let me tell you, it was romantic!"

"I sent my husband an invitation for dinner and dancing one Saturday night. It was all very formal: 'You are invited ... formal wear ...' It was a great success—he invited me back the next weekend."

"I've learned to let my husband go out on the weekends bowling. Although I hate it, I can't change it. In exchange for his weekends, I get Tuesday night out with the girls. It's not perfect, but..."

"I try to look nice for my husband, because I know it's important to him and he appreciates it a lot."

"I found the more I make my husband feel good about himself, the more he makes me feel good about myself. It's almost like being on a teeter-totter."

Husbands: What We Do to Enhance Our Marriages

"I watch the kids every Monday night and let her go out with her friends. I'm not very good with words—but it's my way."

"I try to remember my wife's birthday. It seems important to her and it seems a good way to tell her I appreciate her."

"I know she likes flowers, and if I really want to get to her, I bring her home a bouquet."

"I just tell her I love her."

"We've been through tough times together, and she's always backed and supported me. I try to tell her how much I appreciate that."

"I take her to dinner and a show. It seems to be our way of saying thank you."

"I care about how she enjoys making love. I try to make it special and not just a hit-and-miss thing."

"I fix dinner once a week to make her work easier and show her that I do care. I do the shopping, plan the menu, fix and serve the dinner, and clean up afterward."

"I clean the bathroom once a week. I don't like it, but neither does she. So it's our way of saying that this is a sharing partnership."

"We make a date once a week. We leave the kids and the house and the dogs and cats behind, and we just go out just like when we were courting."

"I went to birth classes with her when I didn't really want

to. But I knew it meant a lot to her. And, in the end, I got as much out of it as she did."

"I love to see her look nice. She's got a great body, and I go out and buy her clothes and bring them home to her. Some people might not like it, but we do."

"It's not my style, but I know it's important to her, so I try to tell her how nice she looks, how much I care, how important she is to me. That's my way of saying thank you."

"I go out and fix her car. I fix the faucet washer, I fix the plumbing. I know it's not romantic, but dammit, it's the only way I have of saying 'I love you.'"

Your Family's Self-Esteem

One of the most outstanding qualities of a healthy happy family is that the members have a sense of wholeness, of belonging, of specialness, and a feeling of high self-esteem.

How do you instill this sense of high self-esteem in a family? Although there is no one right way, each family has its own special system of showing affection, caring and making their members feel special.

Probably the greatest indicator of how you show affection and caring in your family is the way your parents demonstrated affection and love to you. Think of the ways your own mother and father showed affection to each other and to their children. Think of the traditions in your own family of origin that you want to pass down to your children. While you are at it, think of the things your parents did that contributed to your lack of self-esteem. These are the things that, in moments of stress, you may unconsciously pass on to your own children. When you come to grips with these things, you can consciously choose not to repeat that negative behavior.

Parents: Things We Do to Enhance Our Families

"We work to make each child feel that he or she is our favorite child. We make our home a place where they can come for safety and security."

"Although we have four children, we take each child separately out for dinner and make him or her feel special for the moment."

"Even though I'm a working mother, I arrange my schedule to make it a point to always be home when my children come home from school. I try to spend a few minutes with each child alone to talk over the day."

"We have a weekly family meeting where my husband and I and the kids not only make decisions about who is going to do what the coming week, but discuss problems that anyone is having."

"We always hold hands and say a prayer before a meal. It seems to bring us together."

"We have two rules in our family: never to fight at the dinner table, and never to go to bed without making up. That isn't to say we don't fight, but it is to say we choose the time and place."

"Our family vacations are important memories to all of us. We try to choose a place where we will all have fun."

"Whenever we have a birthday in our house, we let the birthday person plan the day with whatever he or she wants to do."

"I try to give love to my children—not only when I am pleased with them, but when I'm not."

"In our house we allow mistakes to be made without horrible punishment or ridicule. We try to keep a sense of humor about humanness."

"Mealtime is a special time in our house. We try to make sure that everyone is able to talk about his or her day and what went on."

"When someone in our family is sick, we try to make him or her very special, and the patient can order anything he or she wants."

"We take the kids out once a week to the zoo or museum for a special trip."

"Picnics are our favorite. I fix fried chicken, potato salad, chocolate cake—all their favorites—and we just take off for the park."

"Christmas is a special time in our house when we have traditions that we do year after year. Baking old family recipes, decorating the tree, Christmas caroling, midnight mass—all mean a lot to our children."

"We love the outdoors and go hiking every Sunday. Since we have teens, it's a family rule that this is a pleasure and those who want to come along, come along. Those who want to stay home or do something else are free to."

"Whenever my children want me to read to them, I drop everything else and sit down and read any book they want without being in a hurry."

"Church is our favorite family activity. We all belong to some part—my husband teaches choir, I teach Sunday School, and the kids are in the youth group. It has been an important part of our life."

"We go to a cabin every summer. It's been a family tradition for five years now. There is no TV, no radio, no movies. We just talk, play games, play cards, and walk and hike together. We all look forward to it."

"We make a date with our children every Sunday and take them to the park or zoo—they get to pick the place. It is a sacred date in our family, and no one backs out."

"On Valentine's Day we give each other flowers with a note of appreciation and love for what every family member means to us."

"On Christmas we make it a family rule that the only gifts to be given will be handmade from our hearts. These gifts mean a lot more than store-bought ones."

"I have knitted a blanket for each of the children to show them how much I love and appreciate them."

"Camping and singing around the campfire has given our family its best memories."

"My husband has shown each of our kids how to fix their

bikes and cars as they get older. They really feel good about being able to fix their own stuff—and it will be a skill they will use the rest of their lives."

"Our greatest gift to our family has been a sense of humor. When we get together, we can laugh and talk for hours and everyone feels good."

"We have family sing-alongs. Anyone that plays an instrument plays along."

"Cookie baking at any time is a special time in our house. We all pitch in and make Swedish pastry or colachis."

"Christmas is a special time in our house. We always go and cut down the Christmas tree and make Italian sausage from an old family recipe."

"Our favorite traditions are nightly 'rock-a-bye' books, making popcorn, and 'watching' the fireplace."

"At birthdays we make a 'money cake' with foil-wrapped coins put into the batter. Also, at birthdays, Daddy comes home early from work to be at the parties and we show movies of previous birthdays."

"My husband takes us all on an 'adventure.' The rules are that the rest of us don't know where we are going until we get there—otherwise it wouldn't be an adventure. He tells us the appropriate dress and whether to pack a lunch. The rest is a mystery."

"Our five-year-old loves us to tell her stories of what she did when she was a baby or toddler. She loves us to ad-lib stories about a mythical little girl named Rebecca Ann."

"We let ourselves express anger, and then we make up and kiss. It cleans the air and everyone feels better."

"Our favorite time is reading books and singing nursery songs at bedtime. It's a ritual that we all enjoy."

"An important tradition in our family is the lighting of Hanukkah candles, and preparing and eating traditional foods."

"We try never to compare the kids but to love them individually for how unique each of them is."

"We have learned not to take our kids' failures any more personally than their successes—and that has taken us years to learn."

"We try to include the kids in solving our family problems. Also, when they make a mistake, or a wrong decision, we let them take the consequences of their own behavior."

"We've taught our kids the importance of work and thrift. They all get allowances and they all have responsibilities."

"We don't expect our children to adjust or live their lives to suit us. We recognize and respect them as individuals."

"We are open and discuss things about sex and sexuality in our family. As the kids get older I get books at their level that will help them learn about sex—then I just nonchalantly leave them around the house where they can read them at their leisure."

"I love teaching my children about the wonders of the world and everyday things. I do get tired of answering a zillion questions a day, however."

"I love playing with my kids, doing arts and crafts."

"I want most of all to help my children develop a high self-esteem, self-confidence, and a love of life and humankind."

"I always try to treat my child as if he is capable of doing things and then let him enjoy the success—or take the consequences."

"I try to remember that my child is a child—not a miniature adult. I try to see things from her point of view, not mine."

"My greatest gift to my children is to help them understand what happens to them, why it happens, how they can get in control of their lives and how they can learn from experience."

"We try to make our children feel that they make a significant contribution to our family. We listen to even the toddler and try to take him seriously—and make him know that he is an important part of our family and that how he feels is important to all of us."

"I was raised in a family where feelings were not recognized. I try to let my children know that their feelings are real and normal and that what is important is to learn to control how they act rather than how they feel."

"I always try to separate what my son does from who he is."

"I've taken lots of parenting classes and was always frustrated until I learned to take one step at a time, and try out new concepts on little things that I know I will succeed at. Instead of trying to change the whole personality of my children I start with a small thing like allowing them to set limits on their curfew."

"We have learned to accept small success, and there are no 'miraculous' overnight cures. We try to build on each success and not let failures set us back too far."

"Now that I have teenagers I am very careful to allow them to have their own values. They may not agree with mine—but the children do have a right and responsibility to learn to make choices and accept the consequences. I want my children's rooms clean—they do not—and it's a royal battle when I try to make them clean up. Now, I just ask them to keep their doors shut and work on more important things."

"The greatest gift we've given everyone in our family is 'letting go': letting them be individuals, giving each other freedom and trust (and that goes for me and my husband too).

"I love watching my child grow and learn. I love to teach him new things. We go to baby water classes together, and it's the high point of my day."

"My husband takes my son skiing and I take my daughter shopping once a week, and then we trade off the next week. It gives us special times to be alone with each child."

"We fight openly in front of our children. They see us fight, solve problems, and kiss and make up. My parents never did this, and I resent it."

"We take our kids walking, hiking, and camping. We hope to share with them our love for the natural world."

"The greatest gift we have given our family is making our marriage our first priority. Because we know that although they need a father and they need a mother, most of all they need us together."

"Waking up a child to see something special outside: a rabbit in the moonlight on a crust of snow, or the aurora borealis."

"Taking time to look at the stars when coming home at night, no matter how late."

"Keeping the Easter Bunny, Tooth Fairy, and Santa Claus stories alive, even after we all know the secret."

"Never missing a school event that any of the kids are in. Making a big deal not only of their successes, but making a big deal of the courage it takes to take risks even if they lose."

All of the above experiences which parents have shared with us have a commonality. They all speak of making people feel special, feel loved, feel cared for. They all speak of a wholeness, a togetherness, an appreciation of individuality. Together these are the experiences that enhance self-esteem and self-worth. Feel good about yourself!

12

THE POWER FACTOR: RULES AND REGULATIONS

Your family's rules and regulations determine whether the family develops in an environment of peace or of war. Rules and regulations may be the aspect of family life that enables you, as parents, to teach your children how to make decisions and live with their consequences. Or they may be the family's battleground, and all your children will learn about solving problems is how to do battle for the rest of their lives.

What Are the Rules and Regulations in Your Family, and What Do They Mean?

Every family, whether healthy or unhealthy, has rules and regulations. Some are verbal and outspoken in the family, some are understood by part of the family, and some are nonverbal and not spoken and not understood.

When we think about rules and regulations, most of us think about who takes out the garbage, what time the kids are supposed to come home, and who does the dishes. If family life were that simple we would probably have a lot fewer problems.

These are the verbal rules that we put up on the refrigerator and everyone agrees to (more or less). These are the rules in those wonderful books you buy on how to get your children to mind you in three easy lessons (money-back guarantee). Although these are important in every family, and we discuss them, they are not the things that healthy or unhealthy families are actually governed by.

The most productive or destructive of all rules are those that are unspoken, but govern the emotional life of the family. These are the nonverbal rules that tell you whether you can express affection, anger, disappointment, joy, embarrassment, and love in your family. And if in your family these emotions may be expressed, there is also an implicit understanding of who can express them, and when they can be expressed—very touchy stuff!

Who Makes the Rules: Power and Discipline

One of the tasks of parenting is to help children evolve into mature and healthy people who are able to contribute to society in a productive way. Your family is a sociological laboratory where this process takes place. One of the ways you as parents help your children become mature adults is through the rules and regulations you have developed in your family. The value lies not only in the content of the rules, but in the process of how the rules are made and kept. We are talking about power and discipline—very important aspects of any family.

When you talk about the rules that have evolved in your family, you are really talking about the way decisions are made and who enforces them. Who makes the rules, and the how, why, where, when, and what of the rule-making, are determined by the power sources within your family. Power determines what decisions are made, who makes them, and how they are made. Power is the way each member of your family influences the others. It is the way you, the parents, and your children make your thoughts and feelings a force in developing rules and solving the many problems which face all families.

There are a variety of power patterns possible in families. Some develop a pattern of equal sharing in which each member of the family has input into the rule-making system. Other families have developed a dominant-submissive distribution of power in which one member of the family makes all the decisions and the rest of the members are expected to go along. Some families exist in a state of warfare in which all members are vying for the dominant position and none is willing to assume the submissive role. A few families are so confused in their decision-making that no one takes the dominant position; each is afraid of hurting the others.

Several generations ago it was common for families to follow the authoritarian model. The father, who was the sole bread-winner, took the dominant position of power in the family, and the mother and children were in submissive roles. Parents dealt out punishment that was often harsh and humiliating.

Binet, Freud, and Adler influenced American attitudes about children. They saw children as human beings who could be badly damaged by the excessive use of punishment and humiliation. They helped parents to realize that harsh and brutal disciplining did not turn out responsible citizens.

John Dewey, father of our modern educational system, helped parents and teachers realize that humiliation, belittling, and oppressive moralizing do not stimulate children to try harder but only increase feelings of guilt and hostility which may emerge in dangerous forms of behavior. Parents and teachers, horrified by the effects of oppression on children, swung to the opposite side, and, for a period, children were raised in an atmosphere of permissiveness. In some families, children became the masters and parents were afraid that if they asserted themselves their children would feel humiliated and rejected. This situation can also produce destructive and incapable citizens, the very thing parents were trying to avoid.

Today, new parenting techniques have developed which concentrate on mutual respect and shared responsibilities, the bases for democratic living. Children from families with a healthy structure learn to accept the responsibilities of shared power. They learn that part of responsibility lies in taking consequences for their actions.

A healthy family power structure is one in which each individual member shares power. The children learn to become productive citizens and adults, able to function in a democratic society. However, a healthy family does not abdicate entirely to the children. When special decisions have to be made the family can be flexible and submit to the final authority of the parents. The mother and father can also be flexible in their power structure and give in to each other at different times. The consequences of misbehavior have been established previously with the full understanding of the children. The discipline the parents use is humane, clear, concise, consistent, and flexible when possible.

In unhealthy families, power may be extremely rigid and authoritarian, or it may be extremely permissive and free. In authoritarian families, one or the other parent is the leader who hands down the rules at all times and who gives punishment. If the authority figure is the father, the mother appears weak and submissive to her children, who resent her for not being able to protect them against unfairness. If the authority figure in the family is the mother, the children do not respect their father and see him as weak and ineffectual.

This is a stressful system for children, and the stress may be expressed in many ways. Some children may react with poor behavior, poor school grades, or chronic illnesses such as asthma. Others may turn inward and become depressed. Although the autocratic system may work well for your family throughout the early years, it is likely to explode during the family's adolescent stage. If the family has rigid rules about drinking, sex, or even slight misbehavior, the family will be sure to see at least one of the children rebel. If the family rules have been harshly strict in demanding that the child attend church regularly, it will probably find that at least one of its children turns against religion. The child will rebel in proportion and in opposite direction to the intensity of the demands.

Just as insidious and dangerous is the family which, either through fear or lack of concern, has no discipline or rules. The children in this kind of family feel unsupported. If the children rule the family, they never learn the important lessons of responsibility. They may have a warped view of life, and will generally make poor marriage partners and parents themselves. It is common for these children to have school problems, because school is a social laboratory where they make their experiments in living. If they do not learn to respect others, they may engage in antisocial behavior such as vandalism and fighting. Adolescents from "laissez-faire" families turn to drugs and sex as an easy way out of a society they cannot understand or face.

What Are the Spoken Rules in Your Family?

There are many books which advise you on how to get your kids to do what you want them to do. There are classes for parent effectiveness training, active-listening classes, sending "I" messages, reality therapy, and the no-lose method of problem-solving plus the tough love approach, when nothing else works. Although each method has positive aspects and parents will find that one or the other will work at times, any "method" that promises 100 percent success underestimates the resources and the needs of the members of the family.

Rules and regulations in a family are constantly changing, because the members of the family are constantly changing. As parents go through their own life changes, so too does the family as a unit. To be a healthy and vital family, the rules (both verbal and nonverbal) must be evaluated, changed, formed and re-formed, added to and deleted on an ongoing basis.

The issues that most verbal rules and regulations revolve around are rules concerning work and day-to-day responsibilities. One of the tasks of a healthy family is to give the children the information and skills they will need as mature adults. Exposing children to the self-respect and pleasure that come from developing a sense of responsibility is an important part of parenthood. These are skills that a child takes into adulthood.

Every family has different needs. In some families, cleaning bedrooms is a big deal; in some families, a curfew is sacrosanct; in some families, carrying out the garbage becomes critical. The point is, it doesn't make any difference what the rules are; what does make the difference is how the rules are made, who is involved in making them, and why they are being made in the first place—and there must be a firm understanding of the when and where of the rules in your family.

Unhealthy Rules: The Who, What, Why, When, Where, and How

War creeps insidiously into a family if the rules and regulations, slowly built up over the years, are rigid, and have no way of changing as the family members move on in their own cycles of development. Unhealthy rules do not take into account the human qualities of the family members, and may therefore impose rigid and inappropriate conditions. Rules that consistently don't work are those that are laid down by one authoritarian voice without regard to the needs or the commitment of the rest of the family members.

Almost all rules become ineffective at some time in a family cycle, and if there is no built-in way of changing rules, they become destructive and damaging to the whole family unit. A good example is curfew, which consists of elements of trust, letting go, independence, freedom, and learning skills to survive and thrive. This issue begins at the age when the toddler launches out into the neighborhood and ends with his or her becoming an adult. Its extremes commence with the "no" stage and peak in adolescence.

An unhealthy family would innocently (and with all good intentions) deal with the issue as does the Brown family. Emily, age two, begins her exploration of the world around her. Joan, the mother who loves and cares for her child, scolds and slaps her child for moving too far. She puts her in a playpen and keeps her there. As Emily moves into the play and school stage, her mother rigidly sets limits. Emily must come right home after school. If she goes to a friend's house, she must be home at five. When Emily asks why, her mother says, "Because I'm the mother and what I says goes."

When Emily becomes a teen, the parents set a curfew of eight o'clock for school nights and ten o'clock for weekends. When Emily is late, her father puts her in her room and grounds her for two weeks. When Emily stays out until two in the morning, comes home drunk, and talks back to her father, he takes out his belt and hits her across the legs. Emily runs away. The parents are bewildered. What went wrong? When she returns, the family goes to the school counselor. They want a happy family, they want peace, they want to do right by their daughter and their family. The rules they have now are not working, and, in fact, are destructive to the whole family unit.

Although rules and regulations are just one issue, the family will have to sort out who makes the rules in this family, why they are made, how they are understood, and how they can be changed to become more effective for everyone involved.

Healthy Family Rules: Who, What, Why, Where, When, How

Rules and regulations don't need to be the battleground of a family. They can, in fact, be a fertile ground on which parents can help their children learn trust, decision-making, problem-solving, and negotiating. When children are involved in rules and regulations, they develop a sense of self-esteem, importance, and wholeness within the family. I wouldn't be foolish enough to say that when you develop a system of making rules and regulations in your family your troubles are over. Remember, families and family members are always changing. And as you, the parents, move on in your cycle of life, and your kids individually move on in their cycles of development, there will be many times that the old rules no longer work. They will become ineffective and shake the very foundations of your family.

What I am saying is that if you incorporate the information that everyone is changing and will be moving on, that new rules will have to be made, then you will have the understanding and tools you need to advance and grow.

A healthy family has rules that are flexible. They are human and take into account the needs of the children and the particular stage of development that the kids, the parents, and the family are in. The rules of a healthy family are clear and well defined. Family members know who is involved, who is responsible, and what are the consequences. The family members know why the rules are made in the first place. Most important of all, not just one authoritarian person puts down the rules; all the family members are part of the rule-making process.

It is rather obvious that healthy rule-making is a concept that starts even before your children are born into your family. It starts with how you, the parents, made your rules and regulations when you first defined your relationship. It grows when your first baby is born and you must make new rules and regulations concerning your roles within your relationship and within your household. It flowers as your child enters into the independent toddler's "no" stage and begins to interject his or her independence into the family unit. As your child explores outward into the neighborhood and school, more and more limits have to be set. Finally, there is the challenging stage of adolescence, in which your rule-setting processes get their greatest challenge as your child, searching for his or her identity, rebels wildly against you as parents.

If, in your family, you include your child in the rule-making process as early as possible and as reasonably as possible at his or her developmental level and if you continue the process throughout your family life, you will probably raise an adult who is able to participate as a valuable member of society. If you wait until your child reaches adolescence to include him or her in setting rules, you may have a more difficult task on your hands.

Chris is John and Sara's first child. As a toddler he begins to explore the house, and one morning Sara goes into the kitchen to see that he has her pots and pans all over the floor. She takes up all of the pans but three and sits down and plays with her son, obviously proud of his newfound skill of exploration. When Chris tentatively shows interest in exploring the neighborhood, she daily takes him for a walk. As he moves on to school, Sara and John take care to sit down with Chris and discuss safety, and have him help set up rules about what they can expect of him and what the consequences will be if he does not carry through.

As Chris goes into adolescence, both parents have a great deal of trust built into their relationship with Chris. They sit down with him and ask him what he thinks is a reasonable time for all of them to expect Chris to be home after school and on the weekends. Chris sets his own consequences and has agreed that if he is not home at a reasonable hour, he will forfeit his allowance for the week. One night Chris comes home late from a party, and has obviously been drinking. The parents tell him they will all discuss the problem in the morning when he is able to think more clearly. In the morning the family sits down and lets Chris tell what he thinks happened, how things went wrong, what are the consequences, and what he thinks should happen.

Throughout Chris's development he learned how to trust. He felt he was an important member of the family and had a high sense of worth and self-esteem. He learned to be part of the family unit and participate in making decisions and solving problems. Although the parents cannot expect Chris to be the perfect child, because he is in his adolescent stage and is still experimenting, the parents can expect Chris to absorb one more lesson in evaluating and accepting the consequences of his actions.

Discipline

The word "discipline" comes from the biblical word "disciples," meaning "learners." This is an important tidbit to keep in mind when you think of disciplining your children. Think of them as "learners," learners of life skills that include both surviving and thriving as creative and productive human beings.

When, as conscientious parents, you must include disciplining in your responsibility, there are several important things to remember:

1. Don't expect your child to be an adult. Develop an understanding of where your child is in terms of his or her developmental stages. A child of two is very different from a child of eight or ten or fourteen. Your children are striving to formulate their concepts of life and of right and wrong, to acquire self-esteem, and to learn how to fit in and belong, and they must do it in the way that seems best to them.

2. Your children's perceptions are different from yours—and, in fact, different from anyone else's. This is because their perception is based on many complex factors, including sibling competition, developmental stage, and sex.

3. Don't expect your child to react as you or his or her siblings would. Each child is unique and sees the situation differently. Ask yourself, "How is my child seeing this experience?" Try to see it from his or her point of view.

4. Don't punish to express your anger. This only results in making the child guilty and angry. Restructure the events to guide your child toward using the situation to become a creative and productive member of the family.

5. It is actions, not words, that motivate children. That means you should model how you want your children to behave.

6. Don't be sucked into the battlefield. Fighting may feel good for the moment—but it is not productive when you are dealing with children, because they are programmed to win. Even if you think you have won the battle, they will win the war through aggressive techniques (talking back, delinquency, teen pregnancy) or through passive techniques (depression, suicide). Remember, it takes two to fight. As an adult you can choose the time and the place that will yield the most effective results.

7. Be clear, concise, and understanding with your children before they need discipline. They should know what you want from them, and what you will do if they do not follow the rules. If at all possible, include them in making the rules and setting consequences of breaking them.

A last word of advice. Don't expect 100 percent success. Life just isn't like that. The more complex your family structure, and the more children you have in different stages at the same time, the more challenges you will face. But it's important for both you and your children not to give up just because things aren't working at one particular time. Keep trying; hang in there.

Negotiate, negotiate, and negotiate some more. Forgive, forgive, and forgive again. Finally, just accept the humanness of yourself and your spouse and your children. It may help you to remember that children will not stay where they are now in their developmental stage. With your help, they will move on to the next maturity level, where once again they will perceive things differently.

Be just as understanding with yourself. Realize also that you will not stay where you are now, either, but will move on to the next level, and perceive things differently. If you seem to be stuck, don't hesitate to seek help from family, friends, school counselors, or professional counselors. Healthy families know when and where to get help.

Evaluating Your Family's Rules

1. What are the verbal rules in your family concerning work, play, limits, discipline, sex, finances, religion, friends, in-laws?

2. Are spoken rules clear, concise, and understandable, or are they vague, unclear, and only partially expressed?

3. What are the goals of your rules? Do they really do for your family what you want them to do? Can you evaluate them for their effectiveness and their ineffectiveness?

4. Explore how your family evaluates rules. How does your family change rules? How does your family get rid of obsolete rules?

5. Make a list of the rules that are effective and enhance your family skills. Make a list of the ineffective rules that are destructive to your family.

6. As your family grows and changes, look at any new rules that might enrich your family life. How do you go about setting new rules? How do you include all the family members? How do you assure that all family members have the same perceptions of the rules? How they are to be enforced?

Unspoken Rules

The rules that may be the most productive or destructive to families are the unspoken rules that govern the emotional life of the family members. All families have rules about how members can express anger, appreciation, annoyance, anxiety, shame, depression, love, dissatisfaction, excitement, frustration, happiness, hate, irritation, jealousy, pride, humor, fright, tension, sensuality, and sexuality and the many other feelings that make humans human.

The healthier the family is, the more freedom it gives family members to express and share feelings. The more you, as a parent, can express your own deep feelings with your children, and the more you help them express and verbalize their feelings, the better you will be able to share the values of life with your sons and daughters. Unexpressed emotions are the bases of most mental illnesses. Restrained anger results in hostility, depression, and physical illness. Unexpressed love and denied appreciation cause withdrawal or aggression. Repressed sexuality shows itself in overt aggression, inadequacy, or impotency.

In a healthy family, children learn to deal with emotions that are a normal and human part of their life.

Affection

A healthy family is able to express affection openly. Words such as "I love you" are an important part of daily life. Touching, holding, stroking are common elements of the family's lives from the moment of the birth of the first child. Physical contact continues for toddlers, in school, and even in adolescence as backrubs, massages, hugs. Notes of love, bouquets of flowers, taking each other out for a movie, walking hand in hand, an arm around the shoulder are all natural signs of affection in healthy families.

Children from this kind of family feel wanted and loved. They feel good about themselves and about others. When they reach adolescence, they are more able to search for meaningful relationships in sexuality. When they choose a marriage partner, they will likely be able to enter into a stable relationship. When they become parents, they will pass on their lessons well.

Members of unhealthy families are not able to show verbal or nonverbal affection toward one another. They feel embarrassed or stifled if they are asked for a kiss or a hug. Family members may engage in verbal put-downs that are ostensibly to show affection, but only hurt one another. If they try to demonstrate affectionate nonverbal behavior, the other person may be repelled or embarrassed. Because they don't get affection at home, it is common for the children to spend a great deal of time at other places.

When the children enter adolescence, they may turn to the opposite sex for the affection that they crave. These adolescents are vulnerable to any touch or person who can offer affection and are easy targets for predatory individuals or organizations.

Anger

Healthy families are able to deal with anger and give important lessons to their children about expressing their anger openly and productively. Anger is an important and necessary emotion of human life. Anger and how it is expressed is an ingredient of mental health.

You, as parents, are the most important indicator of how the rules will be written in your family on the expression of anger. If your children see that you are able to express your anger and are able to channel it in productive ways, they need no words to tell them that it is all right to be angry.

In a healthy family both you and your children know that not only may you share your angry feelings within the family unit, but you are able to use each other as mirrors to evaluate anger, where it came from, how intense it is, why you are feeling it, and how it came about. When your family members are able to share in anger, you are more able to develop an accurate perception and an effective response. As parents of a healthy family, you are able to model positive channels for anger. A healthy family has tools to change destructive anger into a positive force.

The unhealthy family can be destroyed by either overt and uncontrolled expressions of anger and hostility, or covert and hidden anger. This kind of destruction can manifest itself later in mental illness or acted-out behaviors. Children of parents who are uncontrolled in their response to anger tend to lash out at society. They may behave in aggressive ways, such as getting involved in vandalism or fights, bullying younger children, talking back to adults, or becoming involved with drugs and drinking. Such actions may be ways for children to cover their frustration and open up parts of their personality that cannot come out normally.

Anger is just as destructive if turned inward. Depression is anger that the child turns against himself. Children who appear placid, submissive, and reclusive may be hiding great frustrations and are vulnerable to the relief that drugs and alcohol can bring to them.

Sexuality

The most powerful and dramatic of all unspoken rules is in the area of sexuality. Sexuality is one of the most important and pervasive parts of a person's life. It is also the most hidden, guilt-laden, overplayed, and misunderstood facet of our society. From the moment of birth to the last breath, we are sexual beings. A healthy family will view sexuality as wholesome. Sexuality is a continuum which includes love, caring, trusting, commitment, friendship, humor, and pleasure.

An unhealthy family views sexuality as vulgar and unnatural, and produces unhealthy family members who interpret sexuality on a narrow plane solely involving genitals and sexual intercourse.

The lessons you pass on to your children are most likely the messages you received from your own parents. If your parents viewed sexuality as healthy, you, in all probability, do too, and pass on the lessons wordlessly and effectively. If, on the other hand, your parents viewed sex as sinful and dirty, you, without conscious choice to do differently, will in all probability pass on those same feelings.

A child receives his or her first lesson in sexuality at your perception of his or her birth. Do you remember the experience as positive or negative? How you communicate this to the child is significant. The second major lesson you teach your child is in the touching, caressing, soothing attention you gave to your child in infancy. Your approach to toilet training gives your child a vision of his or her body and bodily functions. A child who hears praise and has fun gets valuable lessons in independence. A child who hears "dirty" and "bad" develops lessons in shame that he or she will carry on into sexuality.

All children explore sexuality during early childhood through play such as "doctor and nurse" or "playing house." How the parents react gives them messages of acceptance or messages of guilt. The early information children receive about sex (from either friends in the street or a caring parent) gives them an understanding, or misunderstanding, that they will carry with them long into life.

Finally, the support the adolescent receives as he or she struggles to come to terms with physical, hormonal, and emotional changes and development will be far-reaching. Our society is bombarded with negative messages of sex from TV, books, magazines, and movies. Myths, misunderstandings, and misinformation are rampant and destructive. Little is said about the richness of love and caring. Children need information and skills from which to make one of the most important choices and decisions of their lives: how they view themselves sexually, whom they choose as a partner, and how they live their sexual lives.

When sexuality is repressed and made negative, the issue will come back time and again as an inhibiting force to the individual. You, as parents, have the power to give your children a healthy view of sexuality.

Power and empowerment, rules and regulations, spoken and unspoken. How do these concepts communicate themselves to family members and become a part of your family? There is no book written on families or family therapy that does not list communication as one of the most significant aspects of a healthy or unhealthy family. Communication is viewed in the next chapter.

13

COMMUNICATIONS: ARE YOU LISTENING?

Now, down to the nitty-gritty. How do all the wonderful things like self-esteem, appreciation, expression of anger, and rules and regulations "happen" in a family? Most take place silently and without consciousness. You, the parents, pass them on to your children as your parents passed them on to you.

There may be some destructive communication patterns, however, that you do not wish to pass on. The first part of this chapter concerns healthy communication patterns of expressing feelings, problem-solving, and negotiation skills. The second part of this chapter is about some of the destructive patterns into which unhealthy families may unconsciously fall.

Communication is both verbal and nonverbal. Healthy communication takes place when the words match the action. Unhealthy communication takes place when the actions do not match the words. When a mother tells her child she loves him while at the same time she pushes him away, she sends him mixed messages. Before you begin to give intellectual information, it is important that you take stock of your emotional inheritance concerning the communication of feelings of anger, affection, and sexuality. Look carefully at those things you learned as a child that made your life more productive and creative, and treasure those pieces of inheritance. Now take a look at those things you want to put aside. Those are the things for you to avoid in your parenting. You will have to make some conscious decisions and efforts here.

Nonverbal Behavior

If you came from a family that showed affection and appreciation naturally, you will, in all probability, pass that on to your children with no conscious effort. If you did not come from such a background, you might want to make a special effort to express your physical affection (as by hugging, touching, massaging). Touch is the most powerful of all forms of human communication. It begins at the moment of birth.

You might also want to concentrate on passing on moments of appreciation ("I love you for nothing special—just for being you") from the beginning. Rest assured that these lessons will not be lost on your children, for when you most need it, they will be able to return the same gift to you.

Lessons of passing on productive nonverbal expressions of anger and disappointment are just as precious to your children. Anger is hard to articulate and destructive to repress. Just recognizing the power of your own anger and the anger of your children gives them, and you, great relief. Anger unexpressed is painful. Anger expressed is normal and human, and its power is reduced when it is once expressed.

And, of course, nonverbal expressions of sexuality are most valuable and memorable. A pat by Dad on Mom's behind (or vice versa) is fun and wonderful. Everyone loves it. A wink, a joke, a bouquet of flowers speak more eloquently of the richness of sexuality than all the crude messages on TV or in popular skin magazines.

Effective Listening

Perhaps the most effective of the nonverbal skills is the skill of attending and listening. When one of your family members has a need or a concern and wants to share it with you, you will recognize this as a golden moment not just to share the problem, but, most important, to share the experience.

Some people are just naturally great at listening. Most people, however, are better at talking and giving advice (both ineffective communication techniques). If you were born in a "listening" family, you probably don't need any tips. If you were raised in a family in which nobody listened, your own family system may benefit by learning the few simple steps for effective listening.

These steps include listening with your body for caring and comfort, listening with your eyes for nonverbal language, listening with your ears for the content of the problem, listening with your heart for feelings, and listening with your intuition for signals that tell you how to best help.

LISTENING SKILLS

Listen with your
- Heart—for feelings
- Eyes—eye contact says you care
- Body—turned foward to listen fully
- Mind—for insights
- Ears—for words
- Mouth—kept shut

Listening with Your Body. When members of your family approach you for help, the first gift you can give them is yourself—your body. Show them you really care about them and their problem by putting down whatever you are doing, and give them your *full* attention. This means no pencils, dishes, telephones, cooking, reading. Turn your body fully toward them, and attend solely to the person. It may mean leaning your head toward them, perhaps touching their hand or arm. Such action will give them confidence to share with you.

Listening with Your Eyes. Eye-to-eye contact is one of the first lessons a baby learns in trust, and it is a skill we carry with us into adulthood. When you establish eye contact and let the person know you are giving your full attention, he or she will be able to trust you implicitly. If you are busy gazing off elsewhere, watching television, checking your watch, or talking on the phone, you are not encouraging confidence in yourself as a listener. With your eyes you can interpret many things that may be more expressive of the problem than the words your spouse or children are speaking. Look for messages in body tension. Look at hands for stress. How do the muscles of the face look? Do you see an expression of anger, depression, loss of hope, sadness?

Listening with Your Ears. Next, listen to the content of what your child or spouse is saying. Is the message consistent with his or her body language? Take note of the intensity of the words and expression: Is it consistent with the verbal message? Many people are unable to articulate or perceive reality as it is. Is the message in keeping with reality, or is it perhaps covering another real meaning?

Listening with Your Heart. Understand the feelings the person is expressing with his or her body and words. What do you sense he or she is feeling? All of the well-intentioned words in the world drop by the way if a person's feelings are not taken into consideration. Listen to the tone of your child's voice. Listen for the intensity of the emotion. Search your own repertoire of feelings. Is your baby mad, sad, tired, or overwhelmed? Is your toddler frustrated or fatigued? Is your school-age child angry or disappointed? Is your teenager frustrated or discouraged? Is your wife angry or fatigued? Is your husband bored or inundated by work?

Listening with Your Mouth. Closed is the best position of the mouth for effective listening. Your children and your spouse don't always want advice. They don't want to hear about your Aunt Mary's similar experience. They want you to listen to and acknowledge their feelings. When they're finished talking, offer the person some validation of what is happening to them:

"It seems as if you are worried about..."

"It sounds as if you are afraid."

"You seem to be a little disappointed."

"You look rather angry to me."
"Are you feeling...?"
"You sure seem excited."
"That has given you a lot of joy."
"You sound happy to me."
"You look quite concerned."
"You sound very tired."
"That must have been very frustrating."
"It sounds like a difficult experience."
"You seem overwhelmed."

When you have examined and evaluated the person's feelings to the best of your ability, let your spouse or child know that he or she has been heard. Always confirm your perception of the situation with your child or partner to be certain this is indeed how he or she feels. Nothing is worse than to feel angry and have someone interpret it only as disappointment, or to feel lonely and have someone observe that you look tired.

Communications: Is That What You Really Said?

There is a difference in verbal communication patterns between healthy and unstable families. In fact, research in this area has been on the graphic difference between the messages that individual family members send out and the messages that individual family members receive. Family therapy was developed on just these subtle differences and has given us some guidelines that you can use to send out healthy messages to your children. We'll try to cover some of the more prominent areas of concern in this chapter.

Expressing Feelings

A healthy family helps its members to recognize and express feelings. Behavior (no matter how destructive) cannot be changed until feelings are recognized and heard. Each member, from the moment of birth, has feelings of anger, affection, frustration, disappointment, joy, fulfillment, betrayal, and discouragement. None of these is wrong; all are appropriate and necessary in life. The only wrong thing is when these feelings are ignored or discouraged.

Healthy parents are able to show their children how to express the many feelings each individual has as he or she goes through life. Families that come to counseling often lack the words to describe the intensity of feelings which overwhelm them.

If your family of origin did not have skills in expressing or describing feelings, you might want to develop your own tools for helping your family. Encourage family members to identify their feelings, and to develop a vocabulary which describes their emotional experiences. Helping them to define their emotions allows them to put their experiences in perspective.

It is amazing how even well-educated (or maybe especially well-educated) people have only a few words in their vocabulary to describe what their souls are sensing. Many people only know how to verbalize sadness, anger, or happiness. Such limitations can leave them with a poverty-stricken emotional life. Review the list below. How many words have you used to describe your own feelings? Make an effort to hear your beloveds' emotions and help them increase their emotional vocabulary. Eventually, you should all be able to discern the wonderful nuances of human expressions.

Anger
Annoyance
Anxiety
Appreciation
Astonishment
Boredom
Contentment
Criticism
Cheerfulness
Delight
Depression
Disappointment

Discouragement
Disgust
Dissatisfaction
Eagerness
Embarrassment
Encouragment
Envy
Excitement
Fatigue
Fear
Frustration
Gloom
Guilt
Happiness
Hate
Indifference
Irritation
Jealousy
Love
Misery
Pleasure
Pride
Relaxation
Restlessness
Sadness
Satisfaction
Shame
Silliness
Surprise
Tension
Wonder

It is usually a relief to family members to be able to use a word that best describes how they feel. Not only is the definition of the feelings helpful for mental health, but understanding the extent, quality, and weight of emotions helps put experiences into their proper places.

There are several suggestions in communications that we can

give you as parents which will help make your marriage and your parenting a more rewarding and learning experience. It may mean putting aside old behaviors (such as giving advice and "psychoanalyzing") in order to be helpful to loved ones as they pass through difficult stages of life.

The next time one of your family members comes running in with hurt feelings (whether it is your spouse or child), contain yourself from giving advice or passing on blame, and listen simply for the feelings that you hear. Even in infancy your baby may not understand your words, but your concern, caring, and understanding will come through the tone of your voice. You will give your baby the first lesson in communication that will last him or her for the rest of life.

"I hear that you are angry."

"I hear your frustrations at being treated that way."

"It must have been very difficult for you."

"I would have been disappointed too."

"It looks as if you are overwhelmed and don't know what to do."

"It sounds like craziness and you are confused."

"I don't blame you for being disappointed."

Effective Listening Strategies Through Your Child's Life Stages

Below are some examples of effective listening and positive messages that will help you give your children their lessons in communication. Put them into words your child can understand. You will be rewarded in later years as your children comfort you during your own periods of emotional distress.

Infancy. "Dear, sweet baby, it sounds as if you are really hungry and feel neglected. I see your tears and fury."

Toddler. "I hear your anger and frustration that you need to have some control over your actions and behavior, and toilet training is an intimate and vital issue."

Play Age. "I know you want to move on into the neighborhood, and it annoys and disgusts you when I set limits on your curiosity."

School Age. "I hear you are really discouraged with school and the unfairness of your teachers. It must be hard to study and then not get good grades. How can I help?"

Adolescence. "It's tough to be a teenager and have some people tell you you are grown-up, and other people treat you like a baby."

Young Adults. "It sounds as if leaving home and making a place of your own is scary and frightening. It's not easy, but we are behind you."

Defining the Problem, or What Is It?

After feelings are expressed, we have to solve the problem. Once the reality and extent of the problem has been established, it won't magically disappear. You don't want it to, for this problem represents just one of the many situations your child must confront in his or her lifetime. As parents, it is important to remember that the content of the problem is not as important as the process you give your children for facing and solving them. Again, use the words which will give the best meaning to your child.

Infancy. "It sounds as if your problem is that you want your food, and you want it now."

Toddler. "Now is the time you and I begin to set limits as we work both on my wishing to put away the diapers and your wishing to assert your independence."

Play Age. "It seems that you and I are having problems. You have a great need to explore the neighborhood, and I have a lot of worries about your safety.

School Age. "School is tough, and you sound as if you really want to succeed. Maybe you don't know the rules of the game; I can help you."

Adolescence. "Let's look at the problem and see if we can put it in perspective. It's important that you find out who you are and who you want to be, and it's important to us that we know you are safe and can help you anytime you need it."

Young Adult. "You have been an important part of our family and we hate to let you go, but we know that it is as important for you as it is for us. Let us know how we can help you."

Clarifying the Dimensions of the Problem, or How Big Is It?

Many times, just describing the problem helps family members realize that maybe the problem isn't as big, as bad, or as difficult as they first imagined. Sometimes the problem shrinks to its proper dimensions and the person realizes that all of the time and the energy he or she put into it just aren't in proportion to its real dimensions. This is probably one of the healthiest steps in family communications.

Infancy. "How hungry are you? When were you last fed? How much did you eat? Are you a little ill? Do you really want food, or do you need your diaper changed, or just a little loving?"

Toddler Age. "You want to do things when you're ready, in your own way, but I'm getting tired of dirty diapers. If you are not mature enough to handle toilet training now, I guess it won't hurt to put it off for a while so that we don't turn the bathroom into a battleground. However, when you have reached adequate maturity, helping to shape your behavior is an important part of my parenting."

Play Age. "You really need to go out exploring in the neighborhood, and I have a lot of worries. First, there is the traffic. Second, I don't trust strangers, and third, I don't have a lot of time to be following you around. Fourth, is your request to explore the neighborhood reasonable at this hour? Fifth, how long do you want to be out exploring?"

School Age. "Oh, it is difficult! Your teachers want you to do homework, you want good grades, and you don't know how to get them. We really understand. It's tough to know how to succeed. How often do you have trouble with schoolwork? How well are you getting along with your friends? Do you feel you have a place to do homework? Is there any way we can help you? Do you think a tutor would help?"

Adolescence. "It looks as if you have a lot to face. You have your friends and they think they're right. You have us, your parents, and we think we're right. School tries to tell you what to do, and you, yourself, are trying to come to terms with right and wrong. It's not an easy time. What is the biggest problem in your life? How many times do you feel frustrated? What can we do to help you?"

Young Adults. "Wow! it must seem overwhelming to you. You have to go out in the world, figure out what you want to be, what you want to do, and with whom you want to do it. The choices are frightening in their implications. Why do you think you are so frustrated? What sort of alternatives do you have before you? When do you have to make the choice? Who do you think can help or hinder you in your decision-making? How can we help you?"

Searching for Alternatives

Probably one of the greatest gifts you have to pass on to your children is the ability to find creative alternatives in solving

---

PROBLEM-SOLVING
NO-LOSE METHOD

1. Clarify problem
2. Explore dimensions
3. Brainstorm alternatives
4. Explore consequences
5. Choose a mutually workable solution
6. Assess what to keep, what to change, what to get rid of, what to add

---

problems. It is important to remember that there is not one right solution to every problem. Your solution for yourself at your time of life, or even when you were a child, is very different from the one that is right for your child at his or her time. Your task as a parent is to help your child search through his or her vast resources and choose the best from the many alternatives that are available. This is a lifelong process, since problems will come and go, but the problem-solving process will always serve a person well.

Infancy. "If your problem is hunger, the solution is easy: We can feed you right now. However, if you just ate, eating may not be the answer. Let's try a few other possibilities. Do your diapers need changing? How about a pin sticking you? Are you bored or tired, or do you just want attention?"

Toddler Age. "We have several choices now. None of them is easy. We can choose to sit you on the toilet and not let you get up until you perform. We can choose to ignore potty training for a while. Or, you can show us when you are ready."

Play Age. "It seems like we have a whole list of alternatives to look over. We could let you roam loose without any supervision, or we could keep you in your playroom and never have to worry about you. How about spending one hour in the play-room and then I'll take you to the park and we will play on the slide? Let's get out your toys and let you play with them. How about if I get a neighbor's child to come over and play with you? Daddy will be home in an hour, and he will take you out for a stroller ride. Grandmother has been wanting to take you to the zoo; this may be a great time. Maybe I will put you in front of the aquarium and let you watch the fish. On the other hand, I can always read to you from my novel, and though you may not enjoy the words, you sure need the attention."

School Age. "Let's sit down and talk about all the things we can do to help you with your schoolwork. We have several alternatives. We could just ignore your schoolwork altogether. Or we could supervise your schoolwork every night. We could choose to let you supervise your own schoolwork, and ask us for help when you need it. How about if you plan to study one hour per night for every hour of television you watch? What about signing up for homework help with your teacher? Hey, what if we buy a new set of encyclopedias? What do you think if I spend one hour a night helping you with your homework!"

Adolescence. "Let's see, our rules for curfew are not working right now. How about taking another look at them? Are they inhuman and unreasonable? How about helping us agree on a reasonable hour? How does ten o'clock on the weekdays and twelve o'clock on the weekends sound? Let's try and make some rules together. What do you think about consequences? That is, if you don't come home at the agreed time, what do you think reasonable discipline should be?"

Young Adults. "There are a lot of alternatives we can look at. Have you thought about college and all that it involves? What about getting a job? Living in an apartment? How do you feel about your friends who are getting married now? What sort of problems do you think that we, your parents, are going to face now?"

Exploring Consequences

No matter what your child and you decide, the process by which you found a solution is the most important lesson you can share. It is important for your child to realize that there is no one perfect answer but many answers to the same problem. The next step to the process is recognizing and considering all the alternatives and the consequences that the child (and you, the parents) will have to face. Looking at the consequences of our actions makes up much of the difference between healthy and unhealthy children.

Infancy. "If we choose to disregard your needs, feed you on a rigid four-hour schedule, or resist caressing and fondling you, we will face the consequences of a child who has not learned the most basic lessons of trust. If, on the other hand, we choose to attend to your needs, give you the most important lessons of loving, cuddling, touching, and feeding, we are teaching you now to love and give love."

Toddler. "If we choose to regiment you to an early toilet training, we may set up our first battle between our will and your will. You may become resentful, toilet-train very late, and feel antagonistic toward us. It is easy for us to lay lessons of shame on you during your toilet-training years—messages that can follow you into adulthood. If we choose to allow you some latitude and choice in toilet training, we may make a friend of you in the wonderful act of learning about responsibility and independence.

Play Age. "There are consequences in letting you go into the neighborhood without limitations; we risk losing you in a traffic accident, or having you disappear into the night, or, even worse, having you kidnapped. On the other hand, the consequence of not letting you explore is to turn out someone who is consumed with fear and guilt. However, the consequences of giving you freedom while offering you our protection will give you the independence and protection you need to survive this stage of life."

School Age. "If we ignore your schoolwork and your successes and failures at school and home, we may be setting you up for a lifetime of seeing yourself as a loser—as a failure. If we spend all of our time closely supervising your work, your success will then become dependent on us rather than on your own efforts. If we help you set up a schedule that you can personally supervise, then you can learn the lessons of work, success, and industry that you are going to need in your adulthood."

Adolescence. "The consequences of setting rigid rules is that they are sure to be disobeyed, and do we want to set ourselves up for war? The consequences of allowing you to do as you please may be that you acquire no goals or skills in problem-solving and decision-making. If, on the other hand, we choose to include you not only in the decision-making process but in the consequence-developing process, we may be able to help you with one of the most important skills of life."

Young Adult. "If we try to tie you down, we may keep you at home. But that just makes you unable to move on into the adult world. You might then exhibit your feelings through aggressive behavior (drinking, drugs) or through passive behavior (depression or suicide). We need to support your move from this home."

Choosing the Solution That's Right for You

Resources, such as time, energy, money, and people, play a part in making decisions. It is safe to say, however, that any decision you make for your child in infancy should be designed to give your child a sense of trust. With toddlers, your decisions should be based on how your children will be given a sense of independence and self-esteem. During the play age, your child needs decisions that affirm his or her initiative while promoting a high sense of self-esteem. School is an especially sensitive place where your child gains his image of himself as a winner or a loser. Any lessons you can give him or her in success and any protection you can give your child from failure will ultimately be rewarded.

During adolescence you will be fully tested. The decisions you make at this time are those which if they are good help to foster your child's ego identity, or if they are bad increase his or her role confusion. And, finally, how you let your child leave your family—with joy and hope for success, or with pain and portents of failure—will be your final gift to your child.

Negotiating

Wait, the ball game isn't over. Just because you chose one alternative doesn't mean that you have to live with it forever. If you see that a course of action is not working, allow your children to see that it can be discarded, and give consideration to other alternatives for solution. If you find that four-hour rigid schedules are not working for your infant, there's nothing that says you cannot change to three- or two-hour feedings, or a demand-feeding schedule. If your toddler is not doing well with toilet training, put it aside for a couple of weeks or months and wait until he or she is ready.

If your play-age child is staying away from home too long and too late, make new rules. If your school-age child is not flowering under a hands-off regime, sit down with him or her and establish new rules which will give the child the support needed.

If your adolescent is staying out past curfew and the original decisions are not working, renegotiate a new set of rules in which he or she sets the consequences.

If your young adult left home in anger either by running away or by staging a huge fight in which you were all damaged, it is not the last chapter. Call or write to him or her. Tell him or her that you understand how painful and important the leaving was, and how important it is to you that you talk some more. Set up a luncheon, dinner, tea, whatever, and discuss new solutions.

Accepting That Which You Cannot Change

There are some times when all of the problem-solving and negotiating skills in the world are not working. In business you might just call it a day and break up the partnership. In families you bring another skill into play: that of acceptance. Sometimes you must accept that your baby is going to cry and there is nothing you can do about it. Or that your child is simply not ready for potty training. Or that you cannot let your child roam at will into a neighborhood of high crime. Or that your child is not an A student; all his or her skills are on another level. Or that your teen is in a difficult stage and you will simply have to wait it out. Or that, as a new adult, your child has to find his or her own way out of the home.

Forgiveness

Probably one of the greatest gifts you can give your marriage and your family is to build in a system of forgiveness. When all else fails, love must take over, and there must be forgiveness if all are to survive. How do you show members of your family that you forgive them, and how do they show that they forgive you? Here are some verbal suggestions:

"I'm sorry."
"I just lost it."
"It was a bad day for me."
"We all make mistakes."
"I didn't mean to hurt you."
"I love you."
"You always hurt the one you love."
"Let's never go to bed mad at each other."

And here are some nonverbal ways to show forgiveness:

A smile
A touch
Holding hands
Changing the subject
A hug
A note

It doesn't make any difference *what* you do, just do it.

14

DESTRUCTIVE COMMUNICATION PATTERNS

We have thus far been talking about adult, mature communication styles. That is to say, the family members approach each other in manner, appearance, words, and gestures as adults. However, as we all know, family interactions between parent and parent and between parents and children are not always ideal and mature. In actuality, no matter what the age, many grown people continue to communicate as rebellious children, fighting over power, or as authoritative parents laying down the law, or as accommodating children trying to please parents, or as nurturing parents trying to placate their children.

Eric Berne in his best-selling book *I'm OK, You're OK* hit home for millions when he described how we and our spouses or children approach communications with old messages running through our heads that can turn a simple message into a bizarre and manipulative tool of destruction. The relatively innocent message "Bring me a glass of water" can be changed when a family member comes across as an authoritarian parent or a demanding child. Although there are times and places to run the parent or child "tapes," persistent use of these can generate communication problems that can be passed down from generation to generation, and insidiously turn a happy family into one of snarling intrigue. But healthy communication patterns can turn the most difficult situations into ones of growth and development.

Levels of Communication:
Parent, Adult, Child

Did you ever get the feeling when listening to your family arguments that the words spoken are so similar each time you argue that if you just turned on a recording you could avoid the senseless effort you seem to be going through?

As if things aren't complicated enough, family communications are muddled even further by the fact that within every discussion or argument each family member enters at several levels. Just reflecting on your own behavior will help you to understand from which level you and others are operating.

PERSONHOOD

PARENT
- should
- must
- ought

ADULT
- information
- choices
- control

CHILD
- anger
- blaming
- pouting
- I want it now

All of us operate from three levels: the "child" that we were born as; the "parent" into which our parents, teachers, and outside authority molded us; and our "adult" state, which we gained through putting everything together and coming up with our own unique mature behavior. Although simplistically described, these states exist in all of us. They come from playbacks of events in our childhood. They unconsciously become part of our communication repertoire and, used unwittingly, can go on indefinitely. That is, unless you recognize and put a stop to their destructive role.

Parent

Have you ever found yourself feeling very impatient and disgusted with the behavior of others? Or do you feel the need to be controlling, powerful, and demanding? Is there only one way that things should be done—your way? Do you use phrases like "You must," "You should," "You will," and "You ought to"? Do you demand and expect others to do as you say? You feel that you are OK, but the rest of the world's inhabitants are real dumbos? This is your parent state.

You received the information of your parent state from a huge collection of recordings in your brain during your early growing-up years. These are the messages your parents, teachers, and others gave you. And these are the tapes you pass on to your own children. Here are all the "shoulds" and "musts" and rules and laws that you heard from "authority." They are the verbal and the nonverbal "no's" and "don'ts." They are also the "yeses" and "do's" without rational judgment.

Whenever you are communicating with your children or your spouse and you hear yourself saying "never" or "always," or are being judgmental or threatening, you are probably acting out your "parent" side. And you will probably bring out the rebellious or perhaps the "accommodating child" in your spouse or child. So if your authoritative parent tape says to your husband or wife or child, "I demand that you bring me a glass of water," you will probably hook right into the other person's rebellious child and he or she will in all probability reply with a pouty "No, I don't want to—get your own glass of water." You may wheedle the child with your placating adult—"Please get a glass of water for your poor overworked mommy." Although you will probably get your drink of water, it is only because you have hooked into the guilt of the other person's accommodating-child tape.

Child

Other times, you may feel small and insignificant, and could almost cry at your disappointments. There are times when you feel as if you could stamp your feet because you want satisfaction, and you want it *now!* These are the times when you may have irrational fears, anger, hurt, and powerlessness. You feel as if everyone else is OK, but you sure aren't. This is your child state.

Your "child" tape has two parts. One is the rebellious child and the other is the accommodating child. When you relate to your mate or children in your rebellious-child mode by saying, "I want a drink and I want it now," you usually bring out the "authoritative adult" in them. They may respond, "Get your own drink of water." When you come on as an accommodating child by saying, "Please get me a drink—I was so good to you last Sunday," you usually bring out the "placating adult" in them—"OK, I'll get it this time just to please you."

Adult

There are times when you feel very mature and able to handle matters. Your posture, appearance, and mannerisms match the mature words of wisdom that you have to share. You speak in terms of choice based on realistic information, you take into consideration others' feelings, and you are very effective in your communications. You not only feel OK about yourself, but you feel others around you are OK too. This is your "adult" state.

Where do you get this adult state and how do you know you are in it? Up until ten months of age you were completely at the mercy of your caretakers. However, you began to experience power in reaching out and bringing things to yourself. At the same time you were beginning to crawl and make things happen without your parents. As you began to be in control of your own experiences, you started recording an "adult" tape based on information and judgment of situations.

Your adult tape takes in all the information from the outside, weighs it judiciously, accepts it or rejects it, and makes choices based on reality. The more your parents let you experience reality, the more they allow you to deal with the consequences of your actions and the more they trust you, the more you can depend on the accuracy of your adult tape. When you are in your adult stage, you still hear your "parent's" do's and don'ts, and you can listen to your "child's" feelings and intuition. But, your adult tape has the advantage that you can figure out what is appropriate under the circumstances, and make the best choice for your own individual and unique needs.

Your adult tape keeps your emotional expressions appropriate. Your adult tape checks out and analyzes information and makes decisions based on choices, not emotions. You know you are in your adult state when you make statements such as "I can see that there are many ways to look at this," and "I have made a choice to ignore this," and "After weighing the facts I have decided to move on."

The wonderful thing about the adult tape is that it brings out the adult tape in your spouse and kids, too. And so, to get your glass of water you would probably weigh all the facts, how close you are to the faucet, how tired your spouse or children are, etc. And with an adult statement such as "I know that you are as tired as I am, but since you are closer to the kitchen, would you please get me a glass of water?" you would probably hook into the adult tape of the others. You would probably hear, "Sure, Mom, I'll be glad to."

There is a time and place for all your tapes, whether it be parent (when your child runs into the street and you yank him back), child (when you bubble with spontaneity), or adult. But we do know that in family communications, unconscious use of the child or parent tape to manipulate other family members is almost always destructive and ineffective in healthy communications. There is something almost "magical" in the way that one spouse can bring out a perfectly negative reaction in the other, with much the same intensity.

If one spouse comes on as the authoritative parent—"You

must do this"—the other spouse reacts with his or her rebellious child—"Make me."

When a husband or wife comes on as a rebellious child, it often produces just the opposite in the other spouse, and turns him or her into an authoritarian parent.

Damned If You Do and Damned If You Don't

One of the most destructive games that families can play generation after generation is the Damned If You Do and Damned If You Don't game. It is a game that families use as they pass on mixed messages.

One of the earliest researches in family therapy was by a biologist named Gregory Bateson who was intrigued with the phenomenon of adolescent schizophrenia, a condition in which the adolescent finds reality so painful and confusing that he or she generates an imaginary world that is, at least in the beginning, controllable. Bateson found that families of schizophrenics consistently give out messages that are double-edged— messages that are contrived in such a way that the adolescent could not win no matter what he or she did. When messages are so conflicting and impossible, the adolescent takes the only way out and retreats into a fantasy world in which he or she can control what happens. In this behavior, a response to the Damned If You Do and Damned If You Don't game, the content of the verbal message sent out by the adolescent patient does not fit the nonverbal message.

Game: John comes into the room where his mother is sitting in a chair. She says, "John, come give your mother a kiss." John hears the words and comes over to give his mother a kiss. As he approaches, Mother stiffens up and turns her body away, saying, "Your hands are dirty—don't get them all over my dress." As John turns away, the mother says, "Why don't you kiss your mother? You don't love me." John is damned if he kisses his mother and damned if he doesn't. He is trapped between the conflicting messages. If he responds to the verbal warmth, he has to ignore the nonverbal coolness. If he responds to the nonverbal coolness, his mother denies its validity. It's a crazy world—enough to drive a kid crazy.

Victim, Victim, Who Is the Victim?

Many families appear to outsiders as "perfect" families. The parents and all the children but one appear perfect. But there is one child who always gets into trouble. He or she is the one who is sure to misbehave, fail at school, or even get in trouble with the police. Many times, this family has kept its perfect image only at the expense of one of the family members, whom they all implicitly choose to play the family victim (even the victim agrees subconsciously to be the victim). When the stress of perfection is too great for this family, the chosen victim becomes the family scapegoat, the whipping boy, who agrees openly to suffer the stress of the entire family.

This person, usually the most sensitive child (and very often the second child), becomes the identified victim, while the rest of the family appears to remain stable. This is the child who acts out as a juvenile delinquent, or abuses drugs, or gets pregnant. This is the one who brings the rest of the family into therapy.

Game: Mary is Tom and Ellen's second child. There are four children in the family, but Mary has carried the whole family into counseling, as she is identified by all of them to be the problem. "If it weren't for Mary." "Well, what do you expect?" "She's always the troublemaker." She has dropped out of school and is sexually promiscuous. The rest of the family appears to be normal and healthy.

Counseling sessions show that the father and mother have a cold and unfeeling relationship and have secretly considered divorce. But because the family's reputation is so important, they have dropped the idea. Mary is acting out the hidden stresses and sexual problems within the marriage and has assumed the role of the family troubles. The war between the mother and father is only acted out by the child. She has assumed that by being a troublemaker she can keep the parents together. Their regret at her delinquency is the one thing on which they agree.

The Go-Between Game

The most important bonds that hold a family together are the bonds between the parents. When these are weakened the whole family suffers. Many times the parents with weakened bonds will choose a child as a go-between, and the bonds between the parents become nonexistent as the child takes up the role to pass messages between the mother and father. All members in the family suffer; the parents, the go-between child, and the other family members: the parents, because their relationship deteriorates further; the child, because it is too much responsibility to hold the marriage together; and the rest of the family, because the basic structure is unstable.

Game: Bill is the first child of Joseph and Eileen. During pregnancy, Joseph had begun to feel left out. After the birth, Eileen spent more and more time with Baby Bill and less and less time with Joseph. Strong bonds were developed between mother and son. Father not only felt left out, but really was left out. He didn't know how to fight back and so just withdrew into the background. The next baby was a girl, and Joseph attached to her. Mother and son developed unbreakable bonds in the family. Whenever Eileen had anything to say to Joseph, she would say it through Bill: "Tell your father that dinner is on." "Tell your father that I have a class tonight."

Who Done It?

Blaming is destructive because it undermines the family's self-esteem, and because it does not allow for any constructive learning and growth. Troubled families seem to spend an inordinate amount of time in playing the Who Did It? game. There is no issue that comes up in the family that escapes from the response: "All right. Who did it this time?" Sometimes it is only one family member who consistently tries to point the finger at the perpetrator of the crime, but often it's whole families who turn every issue into one of finding blame.

Game: Andrew comes home with a poor report card and shows his parents. Father looks at mother and says, "It's all your fault. I told you that Andrew could not go out on the weekends if he didn't study, and you let him go anyway." Mother says, "Well, if you would spend more time with your son instead of bowling every Tuesday night this wouldn't happen." Andrew says, "It's not my fault, it's my lousy teacher. She just doesn't know how to teach." No problem-solving, no consideration of what really is behind the poor grades and how to get better grades. Everyone is involved in destructive and demeaning barbs thrown at one another, which are sure to lower one another's self-esteem.

Oh, Poor Me

Another destructive game families may play is the placating game. This is where either one family member or the whole family may be engaged in a game of appeasement at the expense of others' feelings. Many times one of the parents is the placater. "Well, I don't want to hurt your feelings." "Do as you please, and don't worry about poor me." This is a poor game because the family is really being manipulated by a "passive-aggressive" approach that uses guilt or martyrdom to manipulate the family.

Game: The Smith family is engaged in a discussion about where to go on vacation. The father wants to go to the desert; the mother wants to see her family in Iowa; the children want to go to Disneyland. After hearing the other cases for the desert and Disneyland, the mother sighs, "Well, don't worry about me, although my mother is not well and probably doesn't have long to live. I just want to keep peace in the family." Whether the family goes to the desert or Disneyland, how can they have a good time with Mom sighing and moping? The guilt is sure to destroy anyone's joy, and Mom, the martyr, is sure to win one way or another.

The Super-Intellectualizer

Then we have persons and families who do not talk about feelings, who do not face emotional problems, and who spend their time rationalizing, intellectualizing, and pooh-poohing anything that even approaches fear, concern, or worry. They are willing to talk about places and things, and spend a great deal of time poring over world problems and scientific discoveries in the newspaper or *Scientific American*, when what really needs to be faced are problems and feelings within the family.

Game: Regina, the second child, is devastated because no ones asked her to the Junior Prom. She feels unpopular, ugly, and overweight. She is weeping at the kitchen table. Mother says, "Don't worry, Regina—I know several overweight girls who were asked to the prom." Father says, "Regina, with children starving in India, and the threat of the nuclear bomb, how can you cry over such a silly thing?" Regina storms out of the kitchen, saying, "Nobody understands in this family." She is right. Regina needed to have her pain heard. She needed sympathy, and to have her self-esteem bolstered. Instead, her feelings were not validated and her self-esteem was threatened even more.

I Don't Want to Listen: The Irrationalizer

Some people and families who cannot deal with reality or problems may simply ignore feelings and pain by several techniques. A very effective technique is simply to do everything possible not to listen when a person is trying to describe an experience. Reading the newspaper, cooking, watching television, talking on the telephone, all help undermine the problems of a person. Irrationalizing the situation by talking about other unrelated or unimportant events also avoids the problem and gives little comfort to the person's pain. Changing the subject is also an effective way of avoiding problems.

The most effective and destructive way to ignore problems and other people's pain is to get up and slip away, or stomp away and slam the door. Each is effective in making the person feel unimportant, unheard, and destroyed as a human being.

Game: Martha, the mother of three teen children, is feeling overwhelmed with work, housecleaning, and disciplining by herself. She feels she needs her husband to support her when she asks the children to help around the house. After breakfast one morning she broaches the subject to her husband.

"Jim, I'm feeling really tired and angry. The kids leave messes everywhere in the house, and when I come home from work, it infuriates me that I've worked all day and no one is helping here at home."

Jim picks up the morning newspaper and begins to read with great attention.

"Jim, I wish you would look at me, because the house is a mess—and I feel like a slave. I need your support in asking the kids to help me."

Jim gets up, goes to the sink, looks at the dripping faucet, and says, "Hm, looks like it needs a new washer—I'll go get one downstairs." He walks off leaving Martha feeling more frustrated, helpless, demeaned, and angry than ever.

15

UNREALISTIC EXPECTATIONS AND WHAT TO DO ABOUT THEM

There are a lot of myths in our society about the perfect marriage, children, and family which will be sure to be destructive to your family if you believe them. They probably have come from centuries of old wives' tales, and decades of blather about superwives, superhusbands, and superparents. They probably also come from our human desire to be perfect. Well, let's face it, neither you nor your family are perfect, nor are you all going to be perfect. So, our message to wives, husbands, parents, and children is not only to sit back and enjoy yourselves as people, as marriage partners, and as parents, but to allow your spouses and children the same right.

The following myths have created trouble for millions of families. Watch out if you start believing them.

MYTHS ABOUT MARRIAGE

Love Will Conquer All. Love actually blinds the lovers to the vulnerabilities that are real. Making a marriage go takes work, effort, sacrifice, accepting vulnerabilities, negotiating, acceptance, and forgiveness. If you depend on love to conquer all, your marriage will be in trouble.

A Child Will Help a Troubled Marriage. Children put stress on any marriage, but especially a troubled one. If your marriage is troubled and you have a child, not only will your marriage be troubled but so will the child.

I Will Change Him (Her) After Marriage. You married your partner's *total* personality (that means strengths and weaknesses), and after marriage the true and whole personality of your partner will emerge with even greater intensity. Trying to change each other results in resentment and rebellion and is destructive of your relationship.

We Can Overcome Our Differences. It was probably your differences and the way that you cover your insecurities that attracted you to each other. These differences were a lifetime in the making and an integral part of each of you. In the effort to retain your individuality (your essential self), differences are likely to become more intense rather than less as you live and rub against each other.

Romance Will Go On Forever. Romance (that is, blindness to faults) soon falters with living together as each partner's true vulnerabilities and strategies to compensate begin to unfold. Romance is not enough to sustain a healthy marital relationship.

We Won't Let a Child Change Our Relationship. From pregnancy to grandparenting your child will be the elemental factor in changing and moving your marriage relationship. You will both be disappointed and can only fail if you try to keep your relationship unchanged.

Our Dreams Will Remain the Same. As each marriage partner moves on in his or her orbit, your dreams change in terms of occupation, wealth, sex, freedom, and the future. Your dreams may converge, move out, move away—but you may be sure they will change.

We Will Live Happily Ever After. This is the Cinderella syndrome. Even though you may in fact be carried off by a prince, there will still be bumps in the road. This is simply the reality of life. You can depend on stresses from children, parents, money, sex, religion, discipline, freedom, power, expectations, and anger.

Love Conquers/Cures All. Love conquers all as long as you are only showing your good side—and your partner is too. But, when the other side shows itself, as it will, it is going to take more than love to produce a healthy marriage. If you marry to "cure" your insecurities, you are sure to be disappointed to find that you only married a person who shares the same vulnerabilities.

Love Means Never Having to Say You're Sorry. True love means acceptance and forgiveness and forgetting and the ability to say "I'm sorry," when you are not at fault as well as when you are.

Our Marriage Will Be Perfect. Perfection is not for human beings. Expectations that your marriage will be perfect will produce a miserable and disappointing relationship. It is defeating for a couple to believe there will be no problems. Life always has been and always will be full of pain and suffering (along with joy and wonder).

Money Will Not Be an Issue with Us. To anticipate that money will always be available and that you can expect everything (nice house, two cars, furniture all paid for) is unrealistic. On the other hand, to ignore differences in money values is just as destructive and unrealistic. Money is an issue that can emerge as an expression of power struggles, independence struggles, and even struggles with self-esteem. There are few marriages in which money does not become an issue at one time or another.

The Man Always Has to Be Dominant, a Leader. In a marriage where the man is expected always to be the leader, someone else will have to be the follower: the woman. It is predictable that destructive power struggles (even though they may be passive and submissive) will emerge in the marriage.

If My Spouse Loved Me, He or She Would Know What I Am Thinking or Needing. You are two separate, unique individuals who perceive life's experiences in two separate, unique ways. There is no way that you can perceive exactly what your partner is thinking, and trying to do so may get you into deep trouble.

Sex Is a Duty of Marriage, or Sex Is Always Fun. If sex is only a duty, it probably consists only of intercourse, and intercourse is only a part of the whole sexual life of a couple. The kindness, caring, touching, comforting, and pleasuring part of sexuality outside of intercourse forms the richness of a relationship. The sexual relationship of a couple changes throughout their lifetime. Sex takes on new meaning through pregnancy and after birth. As a couple journey through life, they must continually adapt, adding and deleting sexual nuances in their marriage. A couple who expect sex always to be exciting have missed out on the true unfolding of their potentiality for sexuality.

Our Lovemaking Will Always Be Perfect, or We Will Always Be Ready and Willing. All couples experience times in their relationship when the pleasure of lovemaking is not equal or perfect on both sides. Stress, money concerns, pregnancy, illness, fatigue, and occupational pressures all take their toll at some time or another on sexual performance. That may be just the time that comforting, pleasuring, touching, caring, and concern are more important than intercourse. When either partner views the other's inability or lack of interest in intercourse as a personal insult, the results on the marriage can be negative.

He Will Always Take Care of Me. Life is full of surprises. Illness, death, separation, divorce, economic depressions, and disasters are only a few. Today, few people can be certain someone will always take care of them. It is important for both partners to experience independence and freedom.

Marriage Will Fulfill All My Needs and Solve My Loneliness. Marriage was never intended to fulfill all of a person's needs. It is too overwhelming to any marriage partner to become lover, friend, provider, mother or father, counselor, etc. And it is destructive for partners to expect to play all these roles. Real loneliness comes not from being alone, but from being alone in an unhealthy, unloving, incompatible relationship.

Everyone Has to Get Married to Be Fulfilled. Marriage is not for everyone. For a person with a background of an unsatisfactory family life, or one who feels fulfilled through his or her occupation, or one who does not desire a shared life, nothing could be more destructive than the twenty-four-hour-a-day closeness of marriage.

We Will Naturally Love Each Other's Family. Loving in-laws can enrich a marriage immeasurably. Although it is ideal to be able to love or accept your spouse's family, this may not be a realistic expectation. Your spouse's family may be very different from you, their values may differ, and they may not accept you. Insecurities in their own family may be destructive to your marriage relationship. At times you may have to accept that you love your mate, but that your in-laws can be destructive. Otherwise, you may get caught in a dangerous web of game-playing in which you will be the loser.

A Good Marriage Never Has Conflict. A marriage without conflict is an empty vessel. A marriage without conflict does not allow for expression of feelings, for confrontation of real problems, and for exploring and discovering mutual solutions. It does not allow for negotiation or healthy communications. When a couple are able to share their problems, their marriage will grow.

There Is a Perfect Love and a Perfect Relationship. Love is imperfection covered over. The illusion of trying to carry on a perfect relationship does not allow for human imperfections, vulnerabilities, and insecurities. There are many kinds of love and many kinds of relationships—none of them is perfect.

Good Marriages Come Naturally. Good marriages come from a lot of hard work, sharing, forgiveness, and acceptance of each other's abilities and inabilities. Good marriages come from an effort to share power and allow the other person to be his or her own unique self.

We Have to Do Everything Together and Like the Same Things. When a couple feel as if they have to do everything together and like the same things, they become enmeshed in a web of togetherness that does not allow them to express their individuality. One or the other partner may come to resent and subtly sabotage their "togetherness" system. Richness in marriage comes from sharing the sweetness of separateness.

Myths About Parenting

Parents of today are faced with the greatest tasks that have ever been asked of any generation. They are asked to be solely responsible for developing the coming generation without the help of extended families, without the help of concerned neighbors, and without the help of the community. They are being bombarded with "how-to" advice from the experts, and they are constantly being judged by teachers, doctors, and psychologists on how well they are performing. On top of that, mothers are being asked not only to mother but to be an equal part of the earning power of the modern family. Is it any wonder that parents are overwhelmed with the task of parenting? Some couples are even opting out of this huge responsibility. Those who do choose to parent may be crushed by unrealistic expectations of themselves as perfect parents, and their children as perfect reflections of themselves. Here are some particularly destructive expectations parents have shared with me over the years.

I Can Mold My Children to Become What I Want Them to Be. Your children come to you with their own particular strengths and weaknesses. You as a parent can help shape this original material, but you cannot mold it into something its potential won't allow.

There Is Only One Right Way to Raise My Child. Because your children are unique individuals, each child has a separate personality with specific needs and concerns. The proper way to raise that particular child at that particular state in his or her development is the one that seems to be the most successful and brings the healthiest relationship to both the parent, the child, and the family.

I Should Not Let My Children Make Mistakes and Should Shield Them from the Consequences When Mistakes Occur. Your particular task as a parent is to help your children develop the skills they will need to survive and to thrive as they become productive members of society. The only way they can do this is to learn to make constructive choices. This comes from making many choices, learning from mistakes of some of those choices, and facing, with your support, the consequences.

If My Children Are Not Good, It Is My Fault. Your children's experiences with successes and failures are the material with which they build their lives. Their failures are their failures, and they can learn and build on them. Or they can blame you, if you let them. Just as significant, their successes are their successes.

Good Children Never Talk Back to Their Parents. Up until the age of adolescence, your children may never talk back. However, at adolescence there is a physical brain development which predisposes a child to question authority and the status quo. This is built into the human species so that each generation can move on, see old things in new ways and new things in old ways.

My Children Will Be Perfect and Give Me My Second Chance to Be What I Always Wanted To Be and Have What I Always Wanted to Have. Your children carry both parents' genetic codes, mixed to become a new and separate human being. They cannot become your second chance because they are not you genetically, nor do they carry the experiences which made you you. They have their own biological time clocks and cannot do differently no matter how much you want it. Nor should they.

My Child Owes Me Love, Respect, and Total Obedience. As much as we would like to believe it, this cannot be so. Children come into the world without the resources to contract a debt. Children may love and respect you because of what you are and what you mean to them. But to expect total obedience from your children will set up both you and your children for failure.

Parenting Will Be Fun and Easy. Parenting is a tough and arduous task that lasts not only twenty-four hours a day but for the lifetime of the parents. At each stage, the parent must develop new skills to deal with the different needs and problems that each particular stage brings. The parent must be the one in the relationship to offer wisdom and maturity throughout the life cycle of the family.

I Will Not Make the Same Mistakes That My Parents Did with Me. If there is one predictor of parenting it is how you were parented. Unless you consciously recognize those things which you wish to avoid and make a definite commitment to avoid similar behavior, you will in all likelihood make the same mistakes your parents did.

We Will Always Agree on Discipline. Discipline is one of the major conflict issues for couples. Even if you agreed during courtship on general principles of discipline, you will probably find that sometime during the developmental stages of your children you will disagree with each other. Remember, it is not a catastrophe or the end of the world, or the end of your marriage.

We Want to Be Our Children's Best Friends. Your job is to parent your children; their job is to find their own best friends. Children need parents who can give nutrition, protection, and guidance. They need mature role models in their search for their own identity.

Parenting Is a Natural Instinct—Parents Always Know What Is Best and Parents Are Always Right. Parenting is a learned behavior. How you were parented indicates how you will parent. If you were parented well, you will probably parent well; if not, you probably will not. Because of this and the individuality of the child's personality, parents do not always know what is best and parents are not always right. Parenting is a continual process of learning new behaviors, new skills, and new insights; much of the teaching is provided by their children.

Good Parents Have Good Children, and Bad Parents Have Bad Children. Children come in all sizes, moods, behaviors, and patterns. They all change drastically as they voyage through their journey of childhood. We don't choose our children and neither do they choose us. They are who they are, and can behave quite unpredictably.

Parents Never Get Angry. Parents who never show their anger produce children who never show their anger. Anger that is not expressed turns into external hostility or internal depression; both can result in destructive behavior and a painful existence.

When My Kids Are Grown, My Parenting Is Finished. Once a parent, always a parent until death do you part.

Myths Of Personhood

Although the structure of the family rests on the foundation of the marriage, the architects of the marriage are the woman and the man. A marriage cannot be healthy without the intact health of the individuals. As we have seen before, individuals seem to be attracted to others who share the same insecurities in the areas of self-esteem, power, independence, and sexuality. Two people who have self-esteem, a shared sense of power, adequate independence, and healthy sexuality seem to attract each other. Two people who share low self-esteem, an unbalanced sense of power, inadequately developed independence, and confused sexuality also seem to attract each other.

The secret to a healthy marriage is that both partners are working to develop high self-esteem, shared power, independence, and a healthy development of sexual expression. One of the most important aspects of a healthy individual is the wisdom of realistic expectations for oneself.

Unfortunately, it is easy to get caught up in society's expectations for the "perfect" person. These kinds of unrealistic expectations can and do get people into all kinds of trouble, resulting in painful experiences and, often, ultimate failure.

Everyone Must (Should) Love (Like) Me—I Must Have Love and Approval from All the People I Find Significant. You may expect love and approval all of the time from some of the people who are important to you, and you may expect love and approval some of the time from all of the people you find significant. But you will be setting yourself up for failure and victimization if you base your happiness on love and approval from all of the people all of the time.

I Must Always Be Perfect and Unfailingly Competent in Everything I Do. This is a trap that will ultimately drive you crazy as you try to accomplish the impossible.

When Things Are Not as I Would Like Them to Be, It Is a Catastrophe. You cannot be in control of all things at all times. In fact, you cannot be in control of all things even some of the time. When you see things you are not in control of as being a catastrophe, you are setting yourself up for ultimate failure.

If Only I Could Change Others, I Would Be All Right. You cannot change how others perceive, feel, or behave. You can only change how you feel and behave, and how you affect others' behavior.

I Am Helpless and Have No Control Over What I Experience or Feel. Stuck in old patterns and out of control, you are destined to repeat forever old ineffective ways of handling things. Only when you recognize the old patterns and choose to behave differently can you move on to growth and maturity.

I Should Always Be in Control. Persons locked in the never-ending battle of always trying to remain in control of themselves, of their mates, and of their children end up destroying not only themselves, but those around them. Because of the complexity of life, we can never be in control of all things, and can drive ourselves and others to madness when we try.

I Should Never Lose My Temper Because I Could Destroy and Hurt Other People. People are not fragile, and your temper will not destroy them. People can deal with truth. It is the subtle manipulation of silent fury that can maim and destroy. Anger released in mature ways can set the way for growth. Anger held in turns into destructive depression and subtle sabotage.

I Must Always Be Beautiful, Thin, and Attractive, and Have a High IQ. Becoming a slave to exterior beauty and intellectual prowess in hopes that you can hold love and attention gives you an insecure view of your own value to yourself and to others. Inner peace and acceptance provides a profound beauty that will live even after you are gone.

I Must Never Make Mistakes or I Will Not Be Loved. A love that is withdrawn because you make a mistake is a shallow relationship that cannot last. True love lasts because of acceptance of mistakes.

I Must Be a Superperson, Have a Perfect Marriage, and Be a Perfect Parent with Perfect Children to Be Happy. If you view yourself only in terms of what you achieve and how perfect your marriage and children are, you risk losing sight of your own value and destiny. True value comes from and is dependent on your inner self.

I Must Always Be Happy. Life is a series of valleys, plains, and peaks. If you are constantly searching and hoping for the peaks, you miss the humanness and profundity of the plateaus and valleys. If you can accept the deep meaning and importance of occasional sorrow and pain, you will be better prepared for parenthood.

BIBLIOGRAPHY

Adler, A. *Understanding Human Nature* New York: Greenberg. 1946.

Bach, G. & Herb Goldberg, *Creative Aggression* New York: Avon Books, 1975.

Back, G. & Peter Wyden, *The Intimate Enemy* New York: Avon Books, 1970.

Bateson, *Mind and Nature.* New York: E. P. Dutton, 1979.

Berne, Eric. *Games People Play*, New York: Ballantine Books 1976.

Gould, R. "The Phases of Adult Life: A Study in Developmental Psychology." American Journal of Psychiatry, November 1972.

Haley, J. *Uncommon Therapy: The Psychiatric Techniques of Milton H. Erikson, M. D.* NY: W. W. Norton, 1973.

Sheehy, Gail, *Passages* New York: E. P. Dutton, 1976.

Toman, Walter. *Family Constellation* New York: Springer Publishing, 1976.

INDEX